I0011264

Editor's Mind

Secrets from the Chopping Block

Scott Goldman

Table of Contents

Dedication

This book is dedicated to the many who have left us sooner than we would have liked for them to have. While I may never understand the design, I will always honor the designer. Marvin Goldman, Bernard Goldman, Martha Goldman, Arthur Rabinovitz, Bernard Rabinovitz, Belle Bass, Bina Bass, Mitzi Bass, Sut Osofsky, Roz Perkins, Richie Perkins, Andrew Perkins, Elba Aleman, Barry Kaplan and the many others who I may have left off this list...may your light shine eternally. Your essence will live forever in our hearts.

Preface

When I decided to write a book, I was pretty unsure of what I was going to write about. I knew I was going to write about editing and some type of production. When I say some type of production I mean focusing on one area of production rather than all of the areas of production in which I have participated throughout my lifetime. Because, at the end of the day, I have spent time as a professional recording studio engineer, music producer, musician, videographer, video producer, a director, colorist and as an editor. But I think what's important to me to bring across will come through in just about anything I write about being creative and the creative process. At the end of the day that's really what it is. All of these other processes are just that. They are processes. They are processes and channels through which creativity flows.

I believe that creativity comes from the way you look at things and the way you interpret things as well as the way you replicate and represent those things. The presentation medium is secondary. Whether it's shooting video, writing lyrics for a song or playing music, whether it's the mixing of music, or the editing of video...what it really boils down to is creating something that another can relate to. I hope with this book, I am able to do that.

Ultimately, I decided to focus on video editing. Many of my most recognized public accomplishments reside in that space. From television, to movies, to cable and so many more arenas, editing has been my consistent means of expression and livelihood. Of course, there will be some parts of the book that are somewhat just obligatory. For example, I will be talking about some of the basic editing software, as well as talking about types of shots used in videography and other things like that. But hopefully, at the end of the day, the essence of what I'm trying to communicate will come through. And for me, that essence is to trust yourself and trust who you are. Be true to who you are and let that guide you. Let the internal voice go where it wants and then reel it in where you need to reel it in. Don't allow external things to control you. And, don't allow the opinions of others to squash the things you believe in. That's not to say "don't play well with others". And, that's not to say "don't work well with others". And, that's certainly not to say, "don't let other people's ideas share the same validity as your own". It's a creative process and other people are fantastically creative as well. But what I'm saying is trust your instincts. Trust what you feel and trust your vision. That's what gives you your originality. And there is little worse, in my opinion, than losing your originality.

I hope you enjoy this book. As I write this preface, I really don't know what is going to come out just yet because I haven't written it. But as I just said, I'm going to do what I do and trust the process.

Acknowledgment

There are many people I would like to acknowledge not only in the creation of this book, but in my life. There are many people without whose contribution I would never be who I am and where I am. First and foremost, I am thankful to the Creator for giving me the gifts, the tools, the internal spark, and everything esle with which I have been blessed.

Next, I want to thank my parents, my sister and my brother. While they were not always perfect, they certainly did the best they could. But, if they were any different, it is unlikely I would have turned out the way I did. So in this regard, they actually were perfect.

In particular I am thankful for my mother teaching me how to love. This was my mothers greatest gift to me. She definitely taught this by example.

I want to give huge acknowledgment to my wife Magda. She's the one that sees the me that no one else sees. She gets the good, the bad, the ugly, and everything in between. Sometimes she puts up with it and sometimes she doesn't. But I'm sure that's the way it's supposed to be and am fantastically lucky that I chose to fly on that one particular day.

I definitely want to thank my son Arturo. Arturo fills my heart with everything that is magical in the world. God really knew what he was doing with the blessing of children. There is something that happens the first time you look into your childs eyes. It is an indescribable experience. The person Arturo is moves me and moves my heart every day.

I really want to thank and acknowledge my stepdaughter Nathalie. Without Nathalie entering my life I would have never experienced the type of unselfish love that transforms someone from who they thought they were into who they wanted to be. The day this amazing and beautiful girl entered my life, my world changed. Without question, Arturo and Nathalie have driven me to become the man that I am today and that I strive to be.

Professionally, and personally, I will always be thankful to my best friend Marc Serota. Marc is an extraordinarily talented guy. We've been friends since the early days of my life. We have grown together creatively and most every other way.

I also want to thank my friend Larry Rosenbaum who has often been a grounding force in my life.

I want to give special acknowledgment to my earliest creative cohorts. Steve Murphy, Bill Murphy, Mark Knight and, in particular, James Wisner were the most amazing guys to grow up, to learn with, to experiment creatively with, and to just hang out with. I can not overstate their importance in my life.

A very special acknowledgment also goes to Barry Kaplan. Barry was an amazing friend and mentor who left this world way to early. I will forever be watching yours my friend.

If you've been a part of my life for any length of time I wish to acknowledge you as well. I acknowledge the importance of who you are in my life and I thank you with all of my heart

Chapter 1 Get To Know Me

Opening Scene

Born in Brookline, Massachusetts to a modest family, I've had the privilege of living in multiple places. Each has offered me different opportunities to explore and grow. The first of many include moving to a small town in New Jersey named Hightstown. Though I was only three or four years old when we moved there, the town left an indelible imprint on my mind and on my life. I remember it was a pretty small town, but a complete town that had everything in it nonetheless. I don't quite remember the town having tall buildings or substantial shopping malls as they have become familiar sights to see in today's society. But, the town did not need any. It made up for all it had in its own ways. It was the classic small town of an America in the making.

To put it in perspective, Hightstown had only two middle schools and one public high school. But when it came to sports and activities like that, they were plentiful. So all in all, it was a pretty cool place to grow up. The small size of the town meant almost everybody knew everybody, or at least knew their family name. Nobody lived far, and if you had a cool group of friends like I did, you could hang out with them all the time. I had around 5 core friends and around eight other guys who hung out with us pretty often too. We were always playing baseball, basketball, football, capture the flag, prisoners of war, and just about any other sport or contact game imaginable. I mean, we had enough of us to always have two full teams. We basically hung out daily. And on days when someone ditched or was busy with schoolwork, we would invite other kids from neighboring areas to join us and play. They would happily oblige, and we would spend away the entire evening playing with kids that we did not even know a couple of hours before. By the time day transitioned into night we had become well acquainted and had all multiplied our friends. That was the fun of living in a small town. Everybody embraced everybody. We had absolutely no idea what racism was. We had no religious separations. We were just a mixed bag of kids having fun. This was despite the fact that it was still a very divided America at the time. My childhood was very jovial and fun. In fact, it was one of the best times of my life.

Of all the good things living in a small town brought, much of it crashed with a single event. My parents decided to split up when I was around eight years old. Divorces back then were not common yet. So, you can only imagine how the story must have been received by the locals. It spread like wildfire, and lo and behold, I started losing friends.

Some of the friends that I hung out with were not allowed to hang out with me anymore. It was as though their parents thought divorce was like a flu that could be caught and spread around. This was pretty tough to understand as a young kid. But the effect was very real. I remember consciously developing a shell around myself and my heart that would then take decades to put down.

So anyway, at 15, I decided to move to Florida to live with my dad. It was there that I met a guy named James Wisner with whom I got really close. James wrote some of the most amazing music I had ever heard. One day he approached me. He had heard that I wrote lyrics and asked if he could see some. I showed him a few things and he asked if he could take them. I told him that I would write something new instead. So he gave me a tape with a couple of songs without lyrics. They were awesome. That night I played around with a few lyrical ideas and gave them to James the next day. Around two days later, he brought me a tape of one of the songs that he had added my lyrics to. It totally blew me away. The quality of the recording and James' musicianship were amazing. I went back to James' house where he had a full recording studio set up. He played me another of the ideas and sung my lyrics along. It too, was amazing. This was the beginning of many years of a writing and music production partnership. I had had some production experience in my past. But this caused me to rise to a new level. This made me embrace where I was vulnerable rather than try to hide it. In this, I was learning to feel more comfortable and confident in expressing myself creatively. Ever since I was young, I had a particular awareness of my unique creative abilities. Be it a gift or a blessing, I was always able to see things from a creative perspective. Creativity also came very easily for me and I could see infinite angles and options to things.

So anyway, James and I worked together on music. Our individual talents and creativity seemed like a match made in heaven. We were putting out music with passion and a sense of duty. Our music was very well received by our peers as well. We were highly appreciated and our music seemed to really touch people. James was playing guitar in a band called Figment. Figment started playing and recording the music James and I were writing. My not playing in the band gave me a very interesting insight too. Our demo album had became really popular in our school. Though I had written the the lyrics to the songs, I was not playing in the band. So, not as many people knew who I was. This gave me the opportunity to listen to people discuss our songs without knowing I was the writer. It was amazing to see how people would interpret my words in so many ways. It was not that they were trying to understand what I had written. People were bringing their own meaning to the words I had written as my own expression. This was an amazing lesson about art and creativity. This gave me a real license in writing as I was able to strip away any trying to write what people might understand. Instead, I could just express myself purely and let that expression have its own life. I could take the reins off, so to speak. I saw this as an excellent opportunity to explore my creativity without any boundaries.

I carried on making music and then later began to really focus on sound engineering. I dedicated my time to the art of music, and in no time, I was a professional recording studio engineer, producer, and artist. I made sure my creativity knew no bounds, so every now and then I was trying out some new ways of creative expression.

One of my best friends, Marc Serota, was a developing photographer and photojournalist. He was well aware of my writing capabilities. One day he asked me to write articles in context to his photography. It opened the doors to a new creative outlet.

I remember so many times where Marc would ask me if I had anything ready for an imposing deadline. I would reply that it is in progress when I really had not even thought of anything. Then a couple of days later, Marc would remind me that we are closing up on the deadline and if I have something planned or not. I would still be blank, and just before the deadline, when Marc would be totally stressed out over the article, I would sit and allow the entire article to pour out of me in a single shot. It was just like making music. The edits were few if any, and a complete article would emerge. We never ever missed a deadline. Now you may be thinking that I procrastinated, but this was different. Procrastination is when you know you have to do something, but you don't feel like doing it, and then you stress over it until you have to force yourself to do it. And often you end up producing a below average work. With me, it was different. First, I never stressed. Second, I had no difficulty allowing my consciousness to stream into a well—structured article that effortlessly hit its mark. So no, it was not procrastination. It was different. I don't think I can define it. I just allowed myself to tap in when I was ready. I used to think it always came out at the exact moment it was ready and never before. It cooked in my mind until it was ready to be taken out of the oven.

Florida had really played out well creatively for many years. But sometime in my 30's I started to feel like I was in a stagnation period. An awesome friend of mine (and mentor) named Barry Kaplan asked me to go out to Colorado to explore my business mind in a project he was involved with. So I decided to take a well—needed break from the Florida thing and explore some of my untested capabilities. So it was off to Colorado. I was mildly interested in business, and I wanted to explore my creative abilities in that aspect too. It felt like a science project where you mix two unique things and produce something new. So I decided to mix my creativity with business and I got my real estate license. The product I ended up with was discovering my entrepreneurial skills. I learned the ins and outs of real estate and everything related to finance. In the middle of my science project, a client that I had worked for years ago provided me with an opportunity to get involved in video production. How could I refuse? After all, old habits die hard, or in my case, they never actually died. And I immediately took it up. How long could I have stayed away from my true creative nature?

Video production was something exciting for me; to put out your thoughts in moving pictures and edit them so that it conveys your thoughts to people. The whole thing was quite fascinating to me. It was so similar to music in that it was created from nothing. One of my favorite parts of creating music was always the mixing process. This is where you take all of the parts and put it together. You can make almost anything with the ingredients you have created. Video was the same, but with the added visual layer.

I knew now that I had to learn *editing*. I had to be able to be the one "mixing" in the video process. It was what I naturally felt. But I had only used an editor once before. So I grabbed a bootlegged version of Avid Media Composer. I had known that Avid was the industry standard back then. It seemed like until you had mastered Avid you couldn't work as an editor professionally in the film industry. Plus, I also knew it was the most complex to master, and if I could master Avid, I could probably work on anything.

So I took Avid on full force. I took an online course from lynda.com along with material from a few other sites, and I learned Avid. What I realized almost immediately though, was an import lesson. It really wasn't the software or the tools that mattered. They were simply tools. It was the *thinking* that mattered. It was about taking what was in your mind and somehow getting it onto the screen. It all starts with *thinking about it.* It begins in the editors mind.

The next step was learning other video production tools and editing plugins. As soon as I did, I attempted to try out my new skills on an edit. In classic Scott form, I actually learned to edit while producing my first short film. It was my first film ever and my first editing role as well. Somewhat to my surprise, it all turned out really well. It did not look like a first time edit by anyone's standard. In fact, many professionals in the field (many who had been in the industry for a long time) praised it. This was a massive boost for me since it was my first edit (and my directorial debut as well). Those that I told could barely believe that it was my first edit. This was where I really started to understand that if you can see it first, you can create it. It is not about learned skills. It's about what happens in your mind first. It's about trusting yourself. This was how I always operated. It is how I operated in music, in business, in video production, in editing, and in life itself.

I remember creating this one piece with my team. Although we finished it, and it had some great direction to it, we were still a bit lost with it. We did not know what to do with it. It didn't really fit any genre. It didn't do well in any of the festivals I had placed it in. Then one day, I was looking at some upcoming festivals. I saw a film noir festival was coming up and decided to participate in that. But I knew our film was nothing even close to film noir. I would have to make significant changes for it to fit. By changes, I mean, change the entire genre kind of change. So I sat back and totally re-imagined the piece seeing the whole thing in my mind. I went back and made the changes to make a whole new edit in line with nature of the the film festival. I basically chopped the project into a much shorter film. I went with a very film noir style color scheme. I started with a rich black and white theme but with the addition of a single characteristic color smattering. In other words, I emphasized the color red, and every other color was suppressed. I included red where there should be red in the film.

Our star's hair was *red,* the shade of her lipstick – *red*, the apple in the background – *well, of course, red*. There was an emotional emphasis on red. In the end of the film there is even a bloodshot. Obviously, this and the final scene with the apple pulled it all together. It was, in fact, "red" enough in a black and white project. Anyway, I proceeded with submitting this project to the film festival, and it turned out well. It won *"Best Picture, and Best Actress,"* in the only film festival it participated in after the revamp. In fact, this project was the first that earned me the moniker *"Award–Winning"*. And it also taught me a valuable lesson, which was no matter how good the product is, if the market is wrong, the product is wrong. In addition to that lesson, I also learned that editing is about vision. It is about taking your audience on a specific ride. You can make or break an idea with how you edit it. Editing is like a painter with a palette of colors using his imagination and creativity to paint a beautiful picture on canvas. I did the same with my edits; I carried around a palette of video tools and first imagined what I wanted to see and then "painted" the edit until it showed what I wanted it to show. It gave the exact ride I wanted to give from beginning to end. The difference between the original film that did nothing and the new edit that won awards was definitely the fact that the new edit had a clear direction from the onset. I knew exactly what I wanted to do before I set out doing it. This made me realize that everything truly is a product of how you think – it all begins in your mind. The rest is a matter of execution. I am convinced that often times the only difference between a good idea and a bad idea is its execution.

Over the years, I invested myself very heavily into my work — and in my play as well. So much that I almost forgot marriage. That's no joke. But in my 40s, I met a wonderful

24

woman on a plane between Florida and Colorado. My father had been suffering from cancer. I was doing the best I could to take care of him and to spend all the time I could with him for the remainder of his life. That day on the plane, I met my wife and (now) step-daughter, and it immediately felt like my family. It was very "not what I was expecting", nor was that what I was accustomed to. But I just knew.

We were married in 2007. I have an amazing wife and the greatest step daughter who has helped me gain a perspective on life and how beautiful the relationship of a family is. She was quite young, around 7 or 8 years old, when I married her mother. Though she has always maintained (and I always encouraged) a strong and wonderful relationship with her father, she has also embraced me as a father-like figure in her life. This has enriched me in ways I am far too limited with words to describe. In 2009, my wife gave birth to a boy, and he's had the biggest impact on my life ever since. I can't even explain what his birth did to transform my life. In a single moment, my entire soul became different. I stepped into and began living inside of the life I wanted him to see. I have since tried to become the person that would best influence this amazing new person. As I write this today, he is a brilliant, funny, creative, and just totally wonderful person. I'm unapologetically thankful to God, to my wife, and my beautiful children (natural and step) for making my life complete.

I believe that there is a side of life that is undiscovered and unknown; a side that is beyond all the daily sufferings of life, a side that nurtures us and completes us. It defines the relationship between you and whatever guiding principle you hold for yourself. I believe that It is essential to find your own anchor and to build yourself emotionally and spiritually such that you can sail through the storm of life with courage, bravery, gratitude, and compassion. Yes, I believe gratitude and compassion are as central as breathing. The more years I experience the more this truth reveals itself.

From a personal standpoint, I say visualize your life and what you want it to be. Choose who you are and choose who you wish to be. Don't let your lifes influences choose for you. Make your own choice and then take the steps and make the decisions that are required to go step by step into that journey. It may be hard, but hold fast to your truths. Teach yourself to be kind, loving, compassionate, humble, and better today than you were yesterday. Never take this moment for granted.

Chapter 2 Editors Mind

I knew that I was blessed with the gift of creativity ever since I was a child. Not only did I look at things differently than most people I knew, but I also approached anything artistic with a sense of curiosity. I was even conscious how of my own creativity was different than most other peoples. Unlike others I knew, I felt that creativity came naturally and easily to me. Even as young as grade school, I could write my papers effortlessly and in "flow". To push my creativity to its fullest, I kept trying out different things throughout my childhood all the way up through school – from making music, to writing articles to finding my way to video production , video editing, and ultimately to directing. My creative mind knew no constraints and I did all I could to help my creative mind to nurture, grow, and learn.

In all of the creative roles I have filled, I think the two places I feel most at home is mixing music and editing video. They are very similar functions in that they both compose the final "picture" with all of the newly created "parts". For me, editing is not only a continual training and challenge for my creativity, but it is also cathartic and mentally soothing. I think I one of the reasons that I enjoy it so much is that it is one of the places that really allows my outside mind to stop. There is so much going on inside of the editing that it forces my brain to focus and almost exclude the outside world. In the space of even the most challenging edit I can find peace.

As an editor, I have seen rapid growth in the industry in terms of editing tools. Today, a multitude of video editing software has become available. All you have to do is search the internet, and you will be bombarded with tons of options to choose from. Whether you are just starting or you are an seasoned editor, your options are plenty. As shooting video has become much more accessible, so has editing. These days almost everyone has an amazing camera right there in their hand. It's their phone. So where there is a issue a solution typically follows. With so much more demand for and the availability of different types of video editing platforms, getting into editing today is much easier than it was back in the day.

I remember when I had first found interest in video editing, there was not much choice when it came to learning the software. Now, this can be either good or bad, depending on the angle from which you look at it. In a way, not having many options can be considered difficult. But it was also good in the sense that since there were not many options, the ones that were available were the same ones being used by the pros in the industry. So if you had any thoughts of being pro, you simply learned on the systems that you would need to use in order to be able to work as a pro. Or, you used the systems that allowed you to transfer your work to a different work environment rather than using a cheaper lesser known platform that limited your work to the system you were using. And with a little effort, some passion, and a creative mind, you could master most platforms. At the end of the day, editing is in your mind. The platform you use is just a tool. Most platforms have the same functions. The better ones may have a few more or have them laid out better. But the concepts transfer to whatever system you are using. Ultimately, as in anything, your drive and ambition multiplied by your talent determines the pond you will swim in.

You must have heard that hard work beats talent, but the magic is putting the talent and hard work together. I was fortunate to have had both. I remember my first edit on Avid Media Composer, which was widely used in the industry at the time. I had zero understanding of how non-linear editors really worked. All I knew was that I was passionate about making a film. I had overseen a few edits on a few commercials and TV shows I had worked on. But I also knew that I had no budget to always be hiring an editor. I also knew that my vision was becoming harder and harder to express. I also knew that if I really wanted to attack the video industry, I had to learn to make money. Knowing how much I enjoyed the creative component of editing, I knew this was my real entry point into the industry. I had to become a competent video editor on a system that was accepted within the mainstream of the industry, I had to master Avid. So I went through several websites to understand and learn Avid, and Dina short time, I had equipped myself with enough of the technical skills required to fake my way through make my first edit. What I quickly realized, is what became a theme in my editing mind. It starts with thinking about it. It all begins with having a vision and a direction and fumbling through whatever obstacles come up in order to get to that vision. So when I finally managed to complete my first edit, it turned out better than what I had expected. In fact it was surprisingly beyond the expectations of others as well. I had formed a video production company with my best friend, Marc Serota. Marc is a world acclaimed photographer. We ventured into video production together at the advent of DSLR technology. We faked our way through our first production and the filming came out great. But it had now become my responsibility to deliver the edit. And I nailed it. Even seasoned pros could not believe it was my first edit ever. To put it simply I had found myself another opportunity to earn money with my creativity.

Anyway, back to what I was talking about earlier. Today, video editors are widely available to anyone with a knack for it. Moreover, the internet is filled with websites offering free and paid online courses making it all the easier for beginners trying to learn video editing. In fact, I believe that today, it is more comfortable and practical to develop any new skill, be it video editing, photography, or any other.

Still, however, I believe that even with all the available resources today, one factor sets apart an extraordinary video editor from an ordinary one. It is the mind of the editor. Or as I like to think of it, the ability to channel the flow. I believe success begins with the mind. I feel that holds true for video editing. To give you a superficial perspective, the digit six can be interpreted by someone as nine from a different angle. Both are right, but the perspective makes the whole difference. It is the same for video editing. No two editors will ever look at a film and edit the same; they will most certainly have their own creative ideas that will shape the theme of the film and, ultimately, the film's message. And that creativity, in particular, defines a successful video editor. I like to steal an idea of Marc's. I don't know if he made it up or not but he likes to say that as a photographer his images are about seeing what others don't see. In editing, I think it is about taking someone. But you either take them where they don't see or you take them exactly where they do see — and it becomes the same. It seems profound in a way.

Now don't get me wrong; I am not saying that all you need to become a successful video editor is a creative mind. There are many successful editors who are technically proficient in such a way as they compliment a good director. They can bring someone else's vision to light in extraordinary ways. While that is certainly true, the marrying of the two—*a creative mind and the technical skills to complement and realize those ideas of the creative mind* is where magic happens. Because without the technical skills, an idea is just an idea. And an idea that cannot be realized is just a thought that eventually fades away.

I have had people ask me throughout my career for tips and suggestions on editing and what software to learn or use, especially younger people that are just starting in the industry. To them, I always say, editing goes beyond the fancy tools. If you are going to be a pro, learn on pro gear. If you are not looking to be a working pro, learn on the most easy software that allows you to do what you want quickly and effortlessly. Even I use different software at different times. But the most important thing is to develop your mind. Allow yourself the freedom of unrestrained vision. If you have the mind for it and the basic knowledge of editing, then you're all set. The software tool is secondary. All it takes is a vision and a little learning to produce an edit that is capable of inspiring (or moving) people. Every production begins in your mind. The rest is how well you communicate your idea to the software and execute the idea. One such example of "it all begins in your mind" from my own experience as a video editor includes, as I mentioned earlier, when I had hit a wall with an edit I had created. We had entered the piece into different film festivals, but it hadn't gotten any traction. It would have been easy to have just given up. But I knew that this piece was good. It had soul. I knew it in my mind that it could reach *some* audience. So with an unbiased and entirely new approach, a little reworking, some tweaking and some luck, a new film was born. A specific film festival was coming up. I decided to change the entire genre and feel of the film to match the genre of the specific festival. Long story short, the film did exceptionally well, winning multiple awards. This did a few things for me. Not only did it officially make me an award–winning producer, director and editor, but it taught me a great lesson. It is not always about the road you see. It is also about the side trails you may miss while paying too much attention to the road you are traveling.. And on those side trails, many an adventure await.

Maybe this very example from my own life helps put in perspective that a flexible and creative mind has more value than any fancy editing tool. Yes, maybe with a fancy editing tool, you can make use of different techniques and textures to make your edit more appealing. But it all starts with the idea. I think that is where most beginners go wrong in the industry. They invest too much money and time into different editing tools without working on allowing their creativity to "dance". And in the long run, that makes all the difference. A good editor understands the scene and develops the atmosphere in such a way that the viewers do not just see the scene, but are in touch with the scene. A good editor takes notice of intricate details such as the actors' expressions, the scene's emotions, the lightning, the movement, nuances in the background and other such tiny details to provide the viewers with a surreal experience. A good editor edits with motivation; he has a goal in mind, a purpose and a rhythm to the edit, even maybe a message he wishes to convey. So he plans ahead and edits accordingly to make sure that the viewers receive that message. This is something no fancy editing tool can ever achieve on its own.

Before I started writing this book, I had laid a rough outline of the chapters and the content. I wanted to organize my thoughts in a way that they do not spiral around when I'm thinking of what to write in the book. In any long term task such as the likes of writing a book, you would find that it is very easy to get distracted and lose track of your thoughts. One day, I came across a quote that caught my attention, and I liked it so much, I decided to incorporate it. As we're discussing mind versus tools, I found it apropos. It is a quote by Robert Hughes:

"A determined soul will do more with a rusty monkey wrench than a loafer will accomplish with all the tools in a machine shop."

I believe that when it comes to mind vs. tools, this quote explains which of the two is more crucial. The main difference between the works of an amateur editor and a professional editor is just how willing he is to realize his idea in front of an audience as creatively as possible with full attention to detail, and total disregard for his own vulnerability. For such an editor, the tools only make his work easier, and his message more understandable. When I had produced my first edit, I had great editing tools with minimal understanding of how to use them. Although I was equipped with the basics that are, of course, fundamentally important, I did not have the experience of knowing what the tools were capable of. All I had control of was my own mind and my own vision. What created my edit was the creativity I allowed my mind to play with and the determination to find a way to create it with the limited command of the tools I had.

If you ask me what makes an edit great, I would tell you that is first the mind of an editor and then how much he invests himself into the intricate features of the film to complement his idea and then his technical ability of how well he can communicate his ideas to the editing software to realize his vision. By these features, I mean all the tiny intricacies that add life to the edit. These features range from camera angle to lighting to color balancing and everything in between. A good editor keeps these things in focus while is working on his edit. He is constantly finding ways to involve the audience in the scene and make the experience captivating. It is important to develop a rhythm for the edit. Switching camera angles as well as experimenting with unique camera angles are also good ways to give your audience a unique viewing experience. Similarly, in a scene that involves a conversation, the knowledge and feel of the appropriate camera angle becomes more crucial.

During a conversation, of course, you typically use a close–up or a medium angle. That is in the books, but a great editor knows when to zoom in and out during a conversation, depending upon the context of the scene. Or, even when to cut to something outside of the conversations participants give the viewer's mind a pattern . Similarly, it is often important to keep switching camera angles in a single scene to make the scene more dynamic. But, of course, it depends upon the content of the scene. Some scenes can say it all with a strong wide master shot that never deviates. Once again, it is all about feel. But generally speaking, the attention span of an audience is short, so to keep them focused, switching angles not only make the scene more dynamic, but it also helps keep the viewers engaged.

As an editor, keeping the audience is the task. But while you are doing so, make sure you do not overdo it and switch angles a bit too much for the scene. The key to editing is creatively playing with the raw material and producing an edit that is comfortable, engaging and fun for the audience. It is important to find each scenes rhythm, flow and motion. It is all in mind. A good editor knows when something is off, even if it looks good on the screen. Then comes the art of actually cutting and editing. One quality of well-produced films includes the smooth transitioning of scenes from one scene to another. Take any award–winning film, and you will see that the transitions happen smoothly, with rhythm, cadence and motion. This enables users to effortlessly submerge themselves into the story without constantly being disrupted by the obviousness of scene changes. Perhaps, I think this is one of the key differences between a well–produced film and an amateur film. In a low standard film, you will often see that the scenes are cut roughly without intention. This can be painful to watch, as it feels weird and uncomfortable.

These aspects can set apart a great edit from an ordinary one. It's execution comes from the mind of the editor. His ability to see the potential in raw footage in the truest sense of what it could become and the knowledge and the skills required to bring it to fruition. I have worked on many edits in my life, all different, all requiring a different perspective and approach. And I have learned that you do not need expensive and fancy tools to make your edit stand out. I think even experience becomes negligible in front of a creative mindset and the skills to keep an audience engaged. It always starts from the mind. and everything else supports it.

Yes, all editing starts from the mind, but if you cannot realize those ideas with skills and knowledge, it stays in mind, and an idea that cannot be realized is often just a wasted idea. So to all the passionate young creative minds out there, I would advise complementing your creativity with dynamic skills, and you will find just how powerful and meaningful an edit can be and how much you can achieve from a single edit. Put the work into it and you will get it back out in multiples. I do believe that editing is entirely about the vision you create. Working with a palette of assets that you have, it is no different than a painter painting, using his colors and having the whole world to paint based on his colors, using his imagination and skills to producing a piece that is not only beautiful to look at, but is purely an art in its own way. Editing is all about what a mind can make of something, and it is quite impressive what our minds are capable of. I heard someone say something one time that really hit me. He said all art is based in the artist expressing his experience of the world in a moment of time. I think editing is a reflection of that as well. You are creating a whole world expressed in the time line of the edit.

Chapter 3 Tools of the Trade

I have talked a lot about video editing and how the passion for video editing and the creative mind required to realize my edits made me the editor I am today. In this chapter, I will be discussing some of the better editing software that is out there, their features, and how their use can affect the quality of the edit as a product.

Editing tools are in abundance today as compared to in the past. However, the most significant rule here that needs not to be forgotten is that tools are just an environment to work; the most important requirement still is your thinking and your own skills. Creativity is most fundamental of all. Unless you have a creative mind and the technical skills required to produce those thoughts, then no tools can help you. There will be times when you will need your skills more than your tools. For instance, once I was editing a short film. It was an avant garde piece written by a marine and former sniper. I had actually written the screen play using this marines poetry. I was using contrasting images to the words that were being used as the films backdrop. For one of the final scenes, I needed a certain emotion and we really did not have it on film. The footage was completely fine but there was something missing. I could not find a piece of footage that had the right emotion to be the climaxing shot of the piece. I knew I had to do something different to create a shot that concluded the main emotional focus. So, I sat back and thought about what all of the characters were feeling at that moment. How could I express all of that in one moment? It came to me in an instant. I decided to superimpose one image on top of another. I put a piece of footage in the shot in an opaque way. I increased the transparency and used the soldier's image from another shot with just a percentage of opacity. So what I ended up with is a piece where the main character is staring into space from the right side of the screen into the left. My superimposed image of her hero (the soldier) was standing at attention, barely visible on the left. It made for the exact emotion I was looking for. It actually made the entire shot look planned. The reason I tell this story is that it wasn't any fancy editing. It was simple. I just used my creativity to determine what I wanted to feel, and figured out a way to bring it across.

Tools for video editing also do have their charm. Back in the '90s, editing software was not given as much attention as it is today. Transitional features of those editors were not as good as the modern ones. Tools today provide great effects and, in addition to this, are easier to use and generally maintain the quality of the video. I will discuss a few of the softwares I have used or have preference toward. The trend of video editing holds much significance in the field of business and marketing too. I don't see this trend going anywhere anytime soon. I have noticed that random people make videos for their Instagram, Facebook, Tic-Toc and other social media. Wherever you turn you will find video ruling the world. I do suggest you up your video editing game a bit if you do it for your Instagram, YouTube channel or other video driven social space You need attractive videos to get people attracted to your content. This will help you gain more followers and subscribers. There are also certain specifications that you will want to pay attention to while editing such as color correction, compression, etc.

I love working with color. You can play with your viewer's emotions in many ways. It totally depends on how you tweak each scene. You can go with brights, darks, diffusion, lens abnormalities and so much more.

You have definitely seen color play at work whether you notice it or not. It's like when you have watched an old western and may have experienced a little hint of yellow creating an older looking sepia tone. Or when a dream sequence appears and the outer edges take on a blurred effect or a diffused and washed out look. This totally depends on your own sense of feel. Once again, you are creating the journey your viewers are experiencing. Remember that every moment of every scene is created. It is then re-created in the edit. Francis Ford Coppola once said:

"The essence of cinema is editing. It's the combination of what can be extraordinary images of people during emotional moments, or images in a general sense put together in a kind of alchemy."

With this quotation, I am not limiting you to the cinema only. I want you to understand the significance of editing as apart from all other aspects of the film. It could be argued that the editing is the most important aspect of the process. Although each piece is equally important, the editing draws it all together and the editor wields the power to change every other component at any moment. Each scene you edit is the opportunity for you to create something new. Editing is a very intricate web of control over the emotions of your viewers. Although I can ramble on about editing nonstop, I have listed below some of the common editing software platforms as of this writing. This is not in any particular order of preference. As far as preference, I prefer Avid, Adobe Premier Pro, Final Cut Pro X, and DaVinci Resolve. I use them all for the unique strengths of each individual one. It seems each excels at something the others do not. More than half of my edits combine two or more of these platforms, along with Adobe After Effects, which could easily have a book unique unto itself.

1) SDC free video editor

If you are a beginner with a passion for editing but do not wish to spend hundreds of dollars on an expensive video editor, then it does not get any easier than this. The versatility of its interface is worth appreciating. Users are offered a variety of objects and effects. The editor is really simple to use, and you can begin practicing editing videos even with basic knowledge of editing. Its drag and drop features and easy to follow instructions make it good for a beginner. Plus, its free..

2) Pinnacle studio

If you want something just beyond simple editing, there is Pinnacle studio. It is easy for hands-on practice and exhibits great performance. Plenty of editing options are available at the pinnacle studio. Like SDC video editor, it also features a drag-and-drop interface. It is easily accessible and intuitive. In terms of functionality ranges and capacity, it has professional quality. Among all the tools available for beginners, Pinnacle studio stands out. Capture your video material, take out a laptop, and just enjoy some amazing effects provided by Pinnacle studio. It offers 360-degree editing and unique effects like stop-motion.

3) iMovie

Mac users are also video editors, right? For the people who want to do basic editing of their videos on their iMac, there is iMovie. It is a top-rated and very user-friendly interface. It does not overwhelm beginners as it keeps things more simple yet still interesting. It has everything a beginner (who is not looking to build their editing skills) may need to create reasonable quality content. You can also create clips, movies, and trailers in 4k resolution.

4) Avidemux

If you want an editor that can run on all platforms, Avidemux is a relatively easy tool to understand and master. A beginner can get a lot of help from this platform. You will get many format choices according to your need. Several video processing features are present in Avidemux. You will get unlimited tasks, many codecs, and much more. Above all, it is a free tool and can help you maintain the quality of your video.

The next few softwares I'm going to list are relatively advanced with higher level features. However, a larger investment amount is required. The investment is totally worth it if you are skilled enough to utilize all the amazing features.

5) Adobe Premiere Pro

If you are familiar with video editing, then you would know that Adobe Premiere Pro is a big-league tool. Its use is widespread among video editing experts and extremely popular in the professional industry. Its popularity grew partly because of its integration with Adobe's other products including Photoshop and After Effects. It is also attributable to the fact that you can get it as part of Adobe's monthly Creative Cloud offering at a pretty reasonable price point. Although it is built on a premise similar to Avid Media Composer, it still stands alone. I would recommend this software to post-production professionals. It's stable, responsive, and contains all the tools you would normally need. It's integration capability with the other Adobe programs can not be overstated.

6) Final Cut Pro X

Final Cut Pro X is now the standard and a must-have for video editing and post-production on Mac OS X. It is very easy to use, and it is probably the most fun to edit with (in my opinion). That does not, however, make it the best. In fact, Final Cut Pro used to have a much better model in Final Cut Pro 7. But Apple scrapped its pro level editor in exchange for a much more accessible pro-sumer model (Final Cut Pro X). On the one hand I think it was a huge mistake for Apple to have given up Final Cut Pro 7. But I suppose that economics are the driving force sometimes and the pro-sumer market is much larger. Anyway, this is an easy program to learn and normally carries a low price tag. It is a great introductory editor for anyone wishing to do great work, without the need for some of the more pro tools. Many of these tools can even be imitated by plugins to one degree or another.

7) Avid Media Composer

Avid Media Composer is (or was) one of the most used video editing platforms in the professional film industry these days and is considered one of the best editing platforms. There was a day when Avid was the industry standard. Nowadays, depending upon what you are looking for your role to be (pro, semi-pro, independent, etc.) Avid is either a must-know or a no-need-to-know. You can do most, if not all of your basic functionalities on Adobe Premiere Pro. But, If you really wish to get deep into editing, I suggest getting to know Avid first. Every other editor becomes easy to learn after using Avid. I used to use Avid most of the time. Now it has fallen to third in my most used list behind Adobe and FCPX.

8) Light Works

Light works is a complete package full of advanced features for skilled and expert users. Using this editing software requires advanced technical knowledge. You can download it for free. However, it comes with a pro version that has better export flexibility and additional features. It comes with an intuitive and simple interface. The software lets the user launch the first project once the registration process is through. Tabs with the tools for editing videos and audios, managing audio/video files and applying different kinds of effects are also present. Access to audio or video stream capturing tool is also granted to the users.

9) Vegas Pro

Vegas Pro was originally developed by Sony. If you are an expert in the industry who specializes in video editing for movies or TV shows, then I think Vegas Pro is one of the better options that you have. Vegas Pro is used world-wide by many professionals. This tool provides you with your dream quality of video results. Its intuitive interface is great. Special effects such as 3D titles can be created relatively easily using Vegas pro. The company is constantly updating the software to meet user needs and standards. Vegas Pro generally provides the most up-to-date options that are important and most demanded in the industry.

1) DaVinci Resolve

For beginners, again, this is a superb option to go with. The way it offers an all in one tool is something every video editor likes. Whether its calibration, editing, or audio post-production, you won't have to go anywhere else outside of DaVinci Resolve. Fundamentally committed to color and post-production, DaVinci Resolve features a wide variety of tools for altering, blending and creating a high-quality video. A key feature to note here as well is that it has built-in highlights for information capacity and venture collaboration. DaVinci also brings excellent and advanced color correction, full non-linear editing, motion graphics, fusion effects, and professional audio tools. One of the great features of DaVinci Resolve is its ability to translate the time lines of other editing platforms. This is an incredibly useful feature for freelance editors who like to edit on a specific platform and yet deliver on another.

This way you can edit with the speed and comfort you need, and still deliver in whatever format your client requires. I must admit to having cheated with this on numerous occasions. Davinci is also a product of Blackmagic, who's quality products speak for themselves. As such, their pro line can sometimes get a touch pricey. But their mid–range line is pretty reasonable. DaVinci also offers a free version for beginners. While it is outstanding for a free product, it obviously does not contain all the features of a paid version.

These 10 tools each have their place whether you are a professional or a beginner. However, video editing has never been a tool game. Don't stick to these tools and assume that industries will hire you, or you will become a great video editor. Use the concept of beauty with brains in your editing. Beauty without brains is nothing in business life. You have to be intellectual as well as presentable. Keep experimenting and don't limit yourself to the tools..

Consequently, video editing is gaining more power these days than in the past. People have begun to feel the need for great marketing. The entertainment industry has raised its standard and has moved from black and white to a colorful world. Back in the 90's and 2000's, video editing was not considered as much of a job earning skill. These days good quality videos and films have taken over the world. Coming up with creative, attractive and well edited videos has become a regular demand for industrialists.

Believe me; as an editor, the world is really open to you. Today, the whole world runs on marketing and marketing through video advertisements, has become a the new normal. Every industry wants to rank their products high. For this reason, industries are in an constant need of good video editors who can help them in marketing their products in an attractive way to get customers. Videos leave a longer impact on people's minds than still images. Videos do what everything you have tried earlier fails to do. Video editing has helped many companies make their products reach the public, and companies are happily embracing the fact that video editing has helped.

However, do not think of video editing as an easy task. Too many people claim to be a pro at editing. But editing is not simply about downloading the tools and adding some transitions. There are plenty of softwares these days that can also automate this process. But true editing is a comprehensive, complex, and time–consuming skill where the significant amendments in the scenes of films, TV shows, and advertisements are created. When I specify that video altering is complex in nature for us nowadays, I realize how troublesome it has been for people who were editing for the past numerous decades. For a long time, I have been a part of this industry and have come up with a statement that although there are many advancements, there are still certain times we experience an entire mind blockage where we cannot come up with ideas that are creative in certain areas. This is just a fact. I am not discouraging you from becoming a video editor. What I do want to emphasize, however, is that honing your skills allows you to be confident when you step into the world of video editing. Your honed skills will allow you the freedom to allow your creativity to take over when needed without restriction. This can sometimes allow you to break through the blocks because you do not have to fight the software as well. But I digress.

Though it is a very competitive landscape out there, the editing field holds many opportunities for professionals as well as younger editors.

Chapter 4 Work flow Approach

My career in editing has taught me many valuable things, and one of them is managing the creative work flow. You know how to master the assets you have, but managing them in the right sense is the key. The art of video editing is no different than painting. Before starting the painting, artists build the complete picture in their minds. And for the painting to look a certain way, every stroke should be applied meticulously and sequentially. I believe that everything is a product of the way you think. And for things to turn out the way you want them to you need to have a progressive work flow free from distractions.

Editing is an incremental process and working within a well organized work flow approach has always helped me by adding a great level of structure to my edits. As an editor, I constantly cycle through acts of addition and deletion of footage to build a final product that matches my vision. My goal always is to connect my piece with the audience. Nothing facilitates that better than an already thought out and tried process that can transform a bundle of raw clips into a masterpiece. Whenever I begin editing, I divide the work ahead into a series of manageable tasks that can be successfully dealt with. But before diving into time lines, I scrub and organize all of the footage. I find it best to create separate folders for different kinds of clips and label each one of them. For instance, if I want to add certain shots after the interval of the video, I organize them all into a single folder. This way, it is easier for me to locate each clip as needed and it saves me time. The next step that comes in process is dropping cuts or shot selection. It is a foundation for a perfect edit. There are different approaches to shot selection, but I carry it out in sequential steps – short clips, the rough cut and the fine cut. The rough cuts, for instance, are an additive process where I utilize the transcript, the production notes and my general feel to make a rough selection of footage. This is where the basic layout and structure of the video starts taking shape.

The rough cut is mostly based on the script. To make sense of your edit, it is necessary to refer to the script because it paints the story that will be demonstrated in the video. According to the given script and production notes, you can make a rough draft or a time line by correspondingly placing selected clips in order. Sometimes, during the process of rough cut, I find it hard to choose between two shots. Whenever this happens, I place both clips next to each other in the time line. This way, it becomes easier to choose the less fitting and redundant clip and remove it. Most of the time, I make this selection based on a technicality, meaning that I remove less technical shots that I know, for sure, won't look good in the final edit. But for me, shot selection is not always about technicality. Although I know that it is hard to use a footage that is not technically shot well, I have had experiences where I have preferred less technical shots over beautifully shot ones because they appeared more fitting.

Once my rough assembly of shots is complete, I watch it several times through. I look for any possible continuity errors and glaring holes that might disturb the flow and structure of the video. At this point, it is evident what errors need to be fixed and what shots need visual support. I want to point out that the rough cut is just the ordered assemblage of the selected shots, and by no means it implies that it is the final look.

The fine cut, however, begins when I am satisfied with the rough cut. In this step, I meticulously place and time out each shot within the time line. This step is called fine cut because this is where the fineness comes into play. To make it look like all the scenes are connected to tell a coherent story, it is important to time the flow of dialogues, conversations, actions, and visuals. The product that comes out after the fine cut is properly structured with every scene at its accurate place. The video after the fine cut follows the sequence of the final project and is often reviewed by the client.

After the fine cut, the video goes through a picture lock. This is the time when I clean the time line and make sure that there are no stray clips concealed anywhere. What happens during picture lock is that the clips are relocated into specific tracks where they go through numerous finishing practices. This step is a groundwork for finishing tasks. When I am done with picture lock, the sequence that I have created with the timing and edits will not change. An effective practice that I have realized is very handy during picture lock is organizing audio tracks. In a way, it helps an editor to work proficiently during audio post–

production. All audio tracks must be arranged in a way that there are appropriate audio handles on each scene. To make it easier, I generally group similar audios. For example, dialogues of a particular character are grouped into the same audio track, providing easy access. Post-production is the next progressive step after picture lock. Audio post-production, visual effects, titling, and coloring, all come under the banner of the post-production work flow.

Next, I come to the step of adding visual effects. The technique, and time taken, again depends on the quality of work required. I work on visual effects after audio adjustments because this way, it is easier to finish the operation smoothly. Visual effects can be both complex and simple from pulling a chroma key to adding breath-taking CGI effects, depending upon required quality and resources. Color correction and color grading is done after adding appropriate visual effects to the video. Color correction is carried out first as it fixes both color and luminescence errors, creating a constant color balance throughout the shot. I think that color correction is the most amazing tool as it can cover lots of color technicalities. To sum up all the facets of color correction in a single chapter is not possible. But I still want to introduce it by saying that it is often the most defining part of an edit. At this stage, what I do is just balance my footage. And what I tend to mean by balance is that using vector scope, I make sure that all the colors throughout my video are balanced properly. The things I mostly check out are white and black balance, color contrast, and that there is no color cast in the entire footage. I adjust and readjust until I am confident that everything is balanced well and flows.

While color correction and grading works on the overall look of the video, the creative color work keeps changing according to the emotional demands of the scene at hand. Every scene allows you to play with ambiance and create a complex web of emotions that are embedded in colors. Finally, titling is the last element of the editing work flow. Titling and graphics are mostly added as finishing touches to the video. Not every editing project requires the use of titling, but it is necessary to wrap up many film projects. The art of titling is long and storied. It has been there since the early ages of the cinema. The producers and directors in Hollywood spend millions of dollars to make their titles look enticing. I spent time and effort in organizing titles for my videos. There are numerous amounts of patterns that you can follow. Titles that go from top to bottom or bottom to top are called "rolls". They are most used in the movies for end credits where the name of each person involved in the production process is mentioned. Titles can also move from side to side and this type is called "crawls". They are named so because they crawl side to side at the bottom of the screen. I often use this type when I do not want to shed too much light on the titles. They are often disclaimers or news headlines.

Moreover, titles can also be added in unobtrusive or faded fashion. They can also be used with graphics such as a field of color or moving images. How titles are going to appear in the video has a significant impact because if the titles are added into the introduction, then the audience interprets what is to come based on this. You can set the stage and let the audience get the clue of what they are about to see. You must pay attention to this part. How do you want the theme to be? Scary? Thrilling? Playful? Funny? The decision makes quite an impact on the overall mood of the video.

If you are working with teams, then sticking by an appropriate work flow approach becomes more essential. As a professional, I find work flows very useful. They play the role of a road map that you are going to follow in case you want to reach somewhere. With teams, it becomes more difficult to manage all the aspects of the editing process. And if I am supervising an editing project, then I would not want my team to wander in circles and lose the actual flow and structure of the work. For things to go smoothly, I need a work flow, and that too, a solid one. The typical work flow that I follow while managing a team is broken down into several steps. I am going to briefly discuss the elements and specifics of each step.

This work flow approach begins with what I call the first pass. In this step, all the raw footage from the cameras is organized into two groups – primary footage and the B–roll footage. The person responsible for this task goes through the jumble of raw shots and sorts them into the specific group. Primary footage, as the name already implies, is the selection of footage that is going to be the main part of the video. For instance, if you are editing the video from a conference, then the shots of the speaker are going to be your main subject. B–roll footage, on the other hand, is supplementary clips that are going to make cut–away shots. For example, shots of the audience intently listening to the speaker. I find sorting videos this way very helpful for several reasons. First, it allows an editor to identify gaps and errors. If there are any technical issues in the shots that need to be fixed, then these problems are identified at the early stage, and it saves me a lot of hassle later. Second, you can identify better shots and drop junk footage, which makes the work flow in the next step much smoother. When my team is done with the first pass, the next step is to create a solid time line, determine objectives, and identify a suitable editing plan. As an imaginative thinker, I always make plans and drafts in my head before communicating them to my team. Before setting up a time line, I decide to clear objectives in my head. In terms of editing, the objectives usually cover the message that is needed to be delivered through the video, the metrics, the look and impression, and technical scenarios. Then I create the best video editing plan considering the deadlines and tools that will be used. I break down this section into smaller divisions that should be tackled step–by–step. As perfect execution of the plan is based on teamwork, the video editing plan is usually drafted by taking suggestions and opinions from other editors.

Then the next step is to create a time line. This step should be meticulously carried out. I consult all the individuals in my team and collect their ideas to carefully layout the complete time line that effectively reconciles with project deadlines. After the definite and concrete plan has been established, the next step is execution. Start by organizing audio and video files along with creating backups. Backups are necessary to avoid unexpected issues that might disrupt the process. Follow a definite structure. Most of the time, I structure my edits into a flow chart starting with organizing videos and audios followed by voice over, background music, sound effects, SRT files, visual effects, and transitions. As a project supervisor, sometimes, I do review and drop cuts during the main edit, and I make sure that the main edit that my team has created is flawless before jumping into post-production tweaks. This way, you can minimize the problems in the first draft that might become big troubles in post-production. Once you are satisfied that everything in the main edit is perfect, you can start your post-production work flow that usually includes adjusting textures, correcting the timings of sound and visual effects, and many other minor edits. Once the first draft of the project is done, I try to collect feedback from my stakeholders because it will give me an idea early on what my client is looking for in the final draft. Although the feedback process is tricky and complicated, it saves you a lot of effort in the early stage if things are not going the way the client wants to. Certain problems can arise during the feedback process such as the inconvenience of the medium. This means that sometimes, large files are difficult to share with stakeholders through emails or drives. If the client is not able to download or view your video, it creates frustration on both sides. To solve this problem, I prefer cloud–based sharing where the client can stream the video online, and there is no need to download it.

The next step is drafting the final video according to the given feedback and sending it again for approval. Once my videos are approved, to avoid the same issue of downloading larger files, I deliver projects in DVD, Kdan Cloud, or FTP server. I have shared some of the most simplified editing approaches that I follow. However, with multiple tasks at hand, I try approaching things differently. But the work flows I mentioned work out great for me most of the time and help me transform a mountain of footage into something that justifies my imaginations. There are tons of work flow approaches that editors around the world are using to maintain the structure of their projects.

Whether I work in teams or as an individual, I have realized that to run things smoothly, an effective work flow approach is usually necessary. It does not matter if you are working on small projects or big blockbusters, organizing the way you are going to approach things will always remain a fundamental step.

Chapter 5 Think About It

Just like any other skill that requires creativity in the world, editing is something that requires professionals to think in advance and brainstorm ideas before putting them into action. Whenever I start working on a project, I do a lot of groundwork before diving into it. You need to have clear aims and objectives in front of you if you want to create something of value. Video editing is a complex process where it is crucial to deliver the intended message with sometimes only a few resources and your editing skills at hand. Being able to effectively communicate the desired message, reaching the right platform, targeting the right audience, and delivering the right kind of emotions within your edits can be delicate.

While dialogues, background music, and visual effects play a vital role in bringing out the best in your pieces, other factors such as color and graphics are equally indispensable.

As an editor, I prefer sitting down, thinking about certain aspects, setting certain goals and creating a basic idea of where I am going before ever heading towards the actual editing station. To create a good edit, it is necessary to start with a good direction. Think about the true intention of the piece that you are going to edit, the platform it will be viewed on, the message it carries, and the audience it will target. Roughly answering these questions in your mind will help you decide on certain editing requirements and perspectives. It will become easier for you to select the tools you are going to use, the work approach you are going to follow, and the resources you are going to need. In a nutshell, thinking about these questions will allow you to set objectives and follow a clear plan. Video editing is just not about mixing some clips and visually telling a simple story. Video editing goes well beyond that. There are plenty of video types out there that are used for different purposes. From music videos to lecture recordings to movies and beyond and each kind has a separate set of features and requires a different kind of attention from an editor. Before starting any task, I always try to figure out the intention of the video, whether it's a simple video telling a certain story, a music video with graphics or live-action, or a technical speech that intends to deliver a reality based message. Making the intention of the video clear in your head will help you structure it better.

For instance, if you are going to work on a music video, you have to pre-plan it a certain way. You have to decide the tools you are going to use, and you would have to organize your work flow accordingly. In a music video, I start by creating a mufti-camera sequence with audio synchronization followed by cutting clips between that multi-camera sequence. There are many things to consider and many questions to ask at this stage. I also like to find good clips where there is beat and rhythm without the singers mouth moving. These can be key pieces for fixing rough spots or empty spots. I then like to edit the beats with markers and fine-tune the cuts. I sometimes add dramatic effects by playing with the speed. If we talk about storytelling videos, they are structured in a narrative style with a flow and rhythm. To make the intent of storytelling stronger in the video, editors likely plan time, sequence, dialogue flow, background music, and colors very scrupulously. An excellent storytelling piece can only be generated by carefully positioning footage the ways that make the most sense. But sense may not necessarily mean going along with a set order. Allow your creativity to blossom.

When I am working on a story, I focus on minor details while editing, such as where to let a character talk or where to leave a pregnant pause. For example, suppose I am working with footage where an interview is taking place. Sometimes I like to keep little "ums" or even slight pauses uttered by the person being interviewed rather than dropping them from the video because sometimes, based upon the context, a little indecision does not harm. Similarly, if you want to create a graphically amazing piece, you may need to prepare yourself to paint beautifully with pixels and/or other tools that add to what was on the film (or video). The things that could be strategized in such videos might include color corrections and color grading along with visual effects. Understanding the intent with which the video is being created and then putting some effort into making that intention clear as day can be critical in video editing.

The next thing that comes into play when I think about the edit is the platform. The understanding that the video is going to be viewed on a certain kind of platform tremendously affects the whole editing scenario. Different platforms require different kinds of precision, quality, and structure. Take YouTube, for instance. Almost every famous YouTuber uses video editing tools to structure their videos. But you might have noticed that the videos that go on YouTube are often differently structured than short films or movies that play in cinemas. If the intention of the video stops with Youtube, you can consider that most people watching may be watching on a phone or smaller screen. Taking this into consideration is important when thinking about the features. Sometimes you have to emphasize things a little differently in order to draw attention whereas drawing the audiences attention to detail is easier the larger the viewing screen. Tools that are often applied are a bit of extra color correction because YouTube videos are often not shot with perfect lightning. This can especially be true with travelogues or vlogs. On-screen graphics are also very commonly used. YouTubers utilize this tool to create a dynamic look at their videos and keep the viewers hooked. Then, there is b-roll. B-roll is always one of the most efficient tools to make videos more fascinating. I often make use of b-roll to simply hide flaws and mistakes in the video. If a person's shot is not efficiently taken and has technical defects, but voice quality is good, then I may substitute b-roll instead to hide the mistake. Change of camera angles, on the other hand, is the soul of YouTube videos, especially vlogs. But instead of changing and adjusting camera angles during the shoot, it can be modified during post-production. If you have a wide enough shot, then zoom in and zoom out can also be facilitated to make the video look more robust.

Cinema edits and TV shows also differ in terms of editing and shooting. They look dissimilar to the viewers because of both lightning and frame rate. Most TV shows are shot with multiple cameras, which leaves more work for the editor as assembling and carefully editing all the shots can become a tricky business. Lower budget films, on the other hand, are often shot with a single camera. Many movie scenes are designed with a three-point light setup that creates intensity and dynamic range in the scene that brings out excellent dramatic effects.

Before signing up for any video editing project, I try to understand the platform where it is going. As a professional, I need to stay updated on these things. And this way, I can easily figure out how much time, efficiency, and resources are required to edit a piece of video. I often structure my work flow based on where the video is going. During the editing process, the effects and tools can alter the basic idea of the video to some extent. Therefore, knowing beforehand what the dialogues, music, or narration is trying to say can come in handy. I believe that editing tools such as color grading and visual effects can change the whole mood of the scene. Sometimes, it happens that a character can't replicate the same amount of emotions that were part of the script. With editing tools, it becomes easier to bring it back. The message of the video and the editing have a close connection. This is the editing process, where the actual idea of the piece starts taking shape. Therefore, I think it is important for editors to first figure out the video's message and then work in close contact with that message to meet the desired results.

In a scene where a strong emotional message is being delivered, editing can play a part in making it more effective as well as play with the heartstrings of the audience. When I'm working on a project, I repeatedly question myself about the presence of a strong theme. If you have a strong theme in a project, then holding onto that point and creating a persona based on that will be easy. A strong theme will remind what the story is saying and why the audience is watching throughout the editing process. To drive emotional impact I like to utilize 6 primary aspects. They are contrast, engagement, wonder, mystery, possibility, and connection. All these elements playing with each other in a scene can create emotional wonders. Contrast, for instance, can be used to show a glimpse of the present vs. future. The element of engagement is usually connected with a call to action. Wonder state can be created with shots of imaginations. Possibility is often created by targeting the demographics. For the most part, the mystery is used in emotional scenes to help create the hook. And the connection is just the feeling of relatability and rapport that you are trying to build..

As you combine these six elements into your scene, your story will start bonding with your audience. This way, the desired emotional impact can be created. I follow this recipe for many of my dramatic edits by asking questions like *what if?*

As the digital world is expanding, more and more businesses worldwide are realizing the power of video. It's not just cinema or TV. Many other fields use video to convey their messages, express their ideas and promote their products. I have been working in this field long enough to realize that our brains are designed in such a way that they process visuals more quickly. While some utilize this aspect as a marketing benefit to target the right audience and capture customers, others use it to connect with the audience on emotional grounds. As an editor, I strongly believe that the importance of recognizing the right audience is fundamental. There is nothing that captures the attention of the audience better than a well-targeted and well-edited video. Just like intention and platform, the audience also affects the foundations of editing.

Moreover, whenever I sign up for a project, I like to discuss with my clients the type of audience they are going to target or are expecting because it creates a significant impact on the whole video production process. Understanding the specific audience can help you craft a better piece that resonates with that audience. The first thing that you can do is to identify the right audience by communicating with your client. Every video is targeted towards a core audience, even if it is a small group of people. Narrowing down your list of targeted audiences will let you set certain goals for your editing procedures. This will help you start working with a clear focus.

Once you have identified your audience, you can try to collect as much insight as you can about them, such as their age, backgrounds, interests, etc. This will help you to shape basic aspects from the very start. For instance, if you are targeting a young audience, that will influence your video's tone and style along with visuals and graphics. Another thing that I believe is more important in editing is understanding the awareness stage of your audience. If you are targeting a more technical audience interested in the video's subject, they are bound to pick minor details, so you have to be more accurate and intricate with your work. Whereas if the audience is unfamiliar with the video's subject, then they are more likely to be comfortable with a simpler yet understandable version.

I was reading about this research the other day, and it surprised me how short the online audience's attention span is. The piece mentioned that around 20% of viewers abandon the video in less than 15 seconds. So, it is crucial to grab the attention of viewers in those 15 seconds. This can become much easier if you know about what is going to captures their attention. I think and rethink about the audience's interests before drafting the video because it is the key. For instance, if your audience is boys between the ages of 16–24, then there is a good chance that they might follow sports. If there is a sports celebrity that you find relevant to your video, you might include it because it might hit their passion points.

Similarly, if you think that your audience loves music, you can brainstorm ways in which you can engage them. If we talk about business videos, then considering your audience's pain points can also benefit you in several ways. Ask the marketing team of the business to share thorough research with you about the targeted audience. Suppose the video will be used for marketing purposes. In that case, a clear and highlighted message in the video about the problems a certain product or service is going to solve will sound very relevant. However, it is not always necessary. Sometimes, you can simply motivate potential customers to find out more about a service or a product that can become a perfect fit for their needs. No matter how finely you craft a piece in the world of videos, if not presented to the right audience, it will have no use whatsoever. Do youn remember my story about the piece I re-edited to fit the specific festival?

Chapter 6 Shot Selection

Shot selection is another one of those aspects of editing that has tremendous importance. And, there are many different approaches to shot selection. You know, for me, shot selection is much more than just finding technically great shots, because you do want to find technically great shots. And a lot of times it's hard to use shots in a scene that don't really have good technicals. Maybe they're shot too dark, maybe they're shot a little shaky, bad white balance, or something else like that. But for me, the shot selection that I'm talking about different. I like to go through an edit and I like to go through footage and look for shots that just strike me. You know, they have something extra to them. These are shots that I can build a story around rather than shots that are part of a story.

And by this I mean I'd rather have a cool shot that creates a mood than a shot that is just a perfectly beautiful shot.

I've used different kinds of shots for all different kinds of things. You might be able to have it, have a great, great shot that's not technically shot well, but find a way to work it into a scene where the way you work it in makes the scene. There might even be ways to use the the poor shooting aspect of the shot to your advantage. You know, I remember I had a scene one time where a guy was a soldier and he was looking forward and standing at attention. But there were some problems. In the footage itself, there was a little there was a little bowing in, in the hood that was used on the lens too. At any rate, it had a weirdness on the on the outer outer edges of the footage, and for the most part was relatively unusable. But I couldn't find another piece of footage that had the same emotion as that soldier the way he was standing, and I knew I wanted it to make a statement in the final part of the scene. So what I was able to do was put the piece of footage into the shot in a very, very opaque kind of way. I actually explained this exact shot earlier. What I did was increase the transparency and I used the image of the soldier composited into another shot to where it was only in like 8% of its opacity, you know, 8% of 100% opacity so all you could really do is see a ghost image of the soldier and it actually made the entire shot because without that it was just a picture of a girl looking in a in a directionoff screen. But here I was able to use that piece of footage with the girl looking off screen and it almost gave the feeling of the girl looking in the direction of and thinking about that soldier. So even though I had a junky piece of footage, it had impact and I was able to use it in a way that created a whole scene. And this is only one example. You can use you know, maybe a close up image that is a little soft or it's a little blurry. Sometimes you can play around with the contrast or maybe even turn color into black and white and really find a way to use a piece of footage that might otherwise technically seem unusable in a way that really accents your entire shot. So shot selection, for me is more than just finding technically good shots. It's really trying to go through the footage and see what shots move me in a way that makes me want to build something around them.

Ultimately, the shots you select will create how your film will be perceived. If we talk about traditional film making, multiple cameras can be used to shoot a single event. Different angles, camera movement, shot size, depth of field, and shot framing are some of the most basic attributes that are considered when selecting a good shot. Actors will play the same scene repeatedly until all of the camera angles seem to click.

Knowing about the different camera angles and perfect shooting positions is important for cameramen, but for editors, it is just as important. Editors are accountable for selecting the perfect shot that will most effectively shape the story and connect with the audience. In the editing phase, the best–fitting shots are assembled to build a scene. And selecting the best shot among the mountain of footage is truly an art. Most of the recorded scenes do not even make it to the final cut because either they don't fit in right or they have technical errors. Sometimes, utilizing a technically loose piece can turn into a real disaster. Yet sometimes it can hit–off. It's not only my personal opinion but I have had experiences in the past where the shots had technical errors, but they made great scenes as I described earlier with the soldier footage.

Selecting a scene based solely on emotional appeal is not a hands–on approach either. Several aspects are needed to be reflected on before putting a shot in place. For shaping a scene, there are certain requirements. Among different kinds of shots based on shot size, camera angle, focus, movement, and mechanism, it's complicated to select a perfect one that goes. To realistically understand the art of shot selection, I first educated myself thoroughly about various types of shots. I organize different time lines based on what I have learned. For example, if I am talking about a scene where two characters are having an emotional exchange, I will most likely want to include the shots where there is a close–up of their faces. It will create an emotional touch that will grab the audience's attention. Talking about shot sizes, there are plenty of them and each are utilized in different conditions. For instance, Extreme Long Shots are filmed in such a way that they make the subject seem far–off or unfamiliar. You might use these shots when you want to specifically emphasize the location. The Long Shot or Wide Shot, on the other hand, is a little bit closer to the subject. Meaning, the subject's whole body will be in view but it will not fill the frame. In a way, there will be a lot of space above and below your subject's body. I specifically use these shots where there is a need of focusing on both the subject and the surrounding imagery. Then there is Full Shot which lets the subject fill the complete frame while keeping the emphasis on the surrounding. Among all other types of shots, Full Shots are used to feature multiple characters at a time. These shots specifically find their use when there are entries of main characters or very jaunty moments are presented. Medium Wide Shots, on the contrary, are the ones that frame the subject or subjects just from the knee up, and this is something that stretches the distance between a full shot and medium-wide shot. The western films from the 1930s and 40s have often featured a Cowboy Shot which frames the subject from the thigh up. This shot was really popular in Westerns for perfectly fitting in a Gunslinger's gun or hostler, giving the character a very daunting appearance. This shot is still being used today in movies. I always find these shots impressive especially for the hero's entry or other action moments. Another camera shot that is good for revealing characters in more detail is Medium Shot. It's similar to Cowboy

Shot but it records the characters from waist up. This way, more emphasis is on the character while also keeping the surrounding in focus. These shots can add strength to scenes where crucial dialogues are being delivered.

I am talking from experience when I say that whenever you want to draw attention to your character's behavior, reactions, or dialogues, you can go for a Close up Shot. The audience should be able to see every feature of your character in case you want to communicate the importance of what they are saying or doing. Close-up shots also bring a level of intensity into the scene and make the audience relate to it. During editing, I immediately know that this is the time for a close-up shot when there is an excessive need of revealing the character's emotions. Close-up shots fill the side of a frame with the character's face. There are different types of close-up shots as well such as the Medium Close Up Shot. In these types of shots, the subject is roughly framed from the chest up, keeping the subject a little distant with full focus on the face. Contrarily, Extreme Close up Shot focuses on certain features of the subject. For example, it often shows an extreme close up of the mouth, eye, or in case of objects, gun triggers. These shots can communicate the minute details about the character's emotions or an object's features. One of the best films of Darren Aronofsky, Black Swan, features various Extreme Close Up Shots but the one where feathers start growing in Nina's back is pretty remarkable.

Among these shot sizes, how would you know which is the right fit for your scene? Well, the first thing I think about while making a selection based on shot size is familiarity. For example, when you meet someone for the first time, you would want to shake hands, have a polite exchange about the weather or something like that. You would rarely want to just jump in and hug them. So, I assume that audience is meeting the characters in person.

For instance, if there is an entry scene, I would want to keep characters at a distance, maybe I will use a cowboy shot or a full shot to introduce them. And I can use close up or medium close up shots later to build the character. Shot size is the most important attribute when It comes to shot selection. Therefore, it should be done carefully. Keep in mind how framing, movement, and focus can affect your scene and how you can exploit a creative shoot for the scene's benefit.

But also remember that you can use a shot for foreshadowing as well. Maybe you use a shot that is far away to start a scene, but quickly cut to focus on something in one of the characters hands. Then, perhaps, jump to a medium shot and then back. It might not have scene continuity, but it gives a quick foreshadowing of what may come. This can be really effective especially if a quick action is coming that can't be otherwise explained.

Camera Shot Framing is another thing to

consider. It is the art of placing the object or characters within the frame in such a way that it composes an image rather than just pointing at a subject. Over–the–Shoulder (OTS) Shots, for instance, show the subject from behind the shoulder of some other character. This way, it becomes a matter of perspective, especially in conversational scenes. These types of shots are best for providing orientation and creating an emotional connection. Over–the–Hip (OTH) shots gives you a similar effect as an Over–the–Shoulder shot. In these shots, the camera is placed in the foreground, out focusing one character's hip. There is not much difference between Over–the–Shoulder Shot and Over–the–Hip Shot except one character is sitting and one character is standing. In a way, these types of scenes help indicate the power imbalance and benefits you in blocking the characters.

Another important thing is the POV (Point of View). Sometimes, certain scenes require the POV of the character to build a connection with the audience. POV shots frame whatever the character is seeing, taking the audience directly into the character's head. I often use POV shots between two other shots; a shot of a character looking at a certain thing, and then a shot that shows the character's reaction. This way, the POV shows what the character sees and the next moment it rolls back to the character's reaction, giving the audience the complete insight into what is happening. This is not dissimilar to what I just mentioned about foreshadowing. Directors and editors have this uncanny ability to choose the right shot for controlling the audience's vision. You can play with perspectives or move locations just to keep the audience hooked. But there is one aspect of shot selection that holds the power of enhancing visual storytelling, and that is the focus. There are various types of camera-focus shots to choose from, but selecting the right one for the right situation is the key. Starting from the most commonly used camera focus Shots i.e. Rack Focus and Focus

Pull. Focus Pull is used to keep the subject within acceptable focus range while moving into various depths within the frame. On the other hand, a Rack Focus is a variation of Focus Pull and is used to shift focus range between two or more subjects. This is a more aggressive use of focus to tell a competent story.

Next in line are Shallow Focus and Deep focus. In a Shallow focus shot, your subject remains in sharp focus while the background imagery is constantly out of focus. It is mostly done to create an emphasis on the subject. In deep focus shots, to the contrary, everything from subject to background is in focus. I mostly add these shots in the video if I want the audience to take in the whole surrounding, including every particular element in the background.

Then there are soft focus and split diopter. While deep focus lets the audience see every possible element within the frame and shallow focus keeps the subject in crisp focus with a blurry background, the soft-focus keeps everything within the frame out of focus. This effect is perfect for showing dreamy scenes. Split diopter is the most tricky as it allows two simultaneous focal lengths. It is possible to achieve a shallow focus in the background and foreground while keeping the center point out of focus. But I will suggest that this kind of camera shot should be used with caution because the human eye can look into deep or shallow focus, but seeing both at the same time is not possible. And it generates an unnatural effect that draws pointless attention sometimes. The angle from which a certain scene has been shot has a great impact on the overall storytelling. It can tell a lot about the characters, objects, and locations. In traditional film making, a single scene is shot from various camera angles as I have mentioned before. Choosing the right angle that affects the story in the best way is a tedious task, but plays a significant role in manipulating the story. For instance, if you want your audience to connect with the characters directly, then choose the eye-level shots. These shots create the most neutral perspective and let the eye lines of the audience connect with the eye lines of the character. On the other hand, if power dynamics need to be depicted, the camera should be focused at the lower height to emphasize power inequality.

Then comes the high angle shot where the camera points down to your subject. It is great for showing both inferiority or down-level imagery such as in the scene of Deadpool where he was sitting at the top of the building and the camera was pointing at him from the top, showing the streets below.

Next is the knee level shot which has been here since the early days of videography. This shot is filmed from such an angle that it shows only the knees-to-shoe of the character. Such shots build a character's superiority very efficiently if it is combined with lower angles. Similarly, ground-level shots are filmed at ground level to show what is happening on the ground your character is standing on. This can be utilized in many different ways.

Aerial shots have always inspired me. They are, indeed, very remarkable too. They can show a wide expense of scenery in a single shot and are perfect for establishing or opening shots. The famous cyberpunk movie, Blade Runner, used them to show the wide imagery of the cityscape. To shoot these kinds of shots has now become relatively easy due to affordable drones. There is now very little need to shoot sky-high scenes from helicopters which can cost many thousands of dollars.

The next aspect on which your shot selection should be based is camera movement. The way a camera moves while shooting a scene has a great influence on what's happening on screen. It can give meaning to the scene and can help the audience interpret certain actions. In my opinion, the camera movement has always been a powerful film making tool that can seriously alter the perspective of the viewer and create a more visceral visual story.

The most common shots based on camera movements are static or fixed shot, dolly shot, zoom lens shot, camera pan shot, camera tilt shot, tracking shot, crab shot, etc. Talking about the most common one which is the fixed shot, I can say that these shots work well with videos of every genre but for comedy, they are exceptionally great because character's dialogues are often the main focus. These shots specifically focus on your subject's movements and behaviors against its environment. These shots can easily be captured by placing a camera on a tripod stand that remains fixed during the shoot. On the contrary, dolly shots are filmed by placing a camera on a dolly mechanism, a specialized cart that can move around and support film cameras.

Chapter 7 The Main Shot

The main video editing process begins with selecting the master shots for a scene. A shot, in simple terms, can be defined as an uninterrupted, short run of the video that will be trimmed or cut to craft an entire scene. And selecting the perfect one that justifies the whole story is a tricky matter. The editor must work closely with the director or client during the whole process of editing to better interpret the motives. Furthermore, an editor views all the shots taken from different camera angles, studies them, and works on them to create a perfect, flawless scene. This is a sequential process that starts from choosing master shots and ends at molding them perfectly into a scene.

I sometimes look at this process like writing a college term paper. You get an idea, you prepare a rough draft, you review the whole thing countless times to make it flow perfectly, and then you create the final version. Similarly, editing is a process that reaches the completion of going through different stages. As I have discussed in the previous chapter that directors use different angles, frames, shot sizes, and camera movements to capture the scene in the most effective way. Different kinds of shots can define the scene differently. The editor must go through all the shots to figure out the main shot that will become the part of the scene, as some of the most legendary scenes in film history are merely products of genius shot selection.

Speaking for myself, I try to become familiar with all the shots based on their dynamics and technicality. Sometimes I keep notes while reviewing shots and write down my responses, ideas, and any thought that pops into my head. I will use a time code to link my ideas to any shot. After consulting my notes, I select the main shots that will become part of my edit. I first create a simpler version with the same kind of shots looped together. This version does not have any specific edits, just a fewer number of shots. I create this version to get a detailed idea about how the story will proceed.

Then I start working on one scene at a time, reviewing all the takes of a certain shot to find out the most consistent material that fits best inside the totality of the scene. This is what editors call the main shot. When all the main shots are selected, and I have created a draft of a good working version of the scene, I place each shot into a particular time line. I save all the timelines that I have made during the selection process in case I want to backtrack or make further changes. During this stage, the sounds that are synced with shots are kept intact, but no additional audio will be introduced as this will be the part of audio post-production which will come later.

I repeat this process with each scene, selecting main shots, and putting them into timelines. I move no further in the editing process until I have looked at each scene individually from multiple timeline combinations.

I remember that I read a quote from Michelangelo somewhere and I think it fits completely in the editing world too. The quote said,

"Every block of stone has a statue inside it, and it is the task of the sculptor to discover it."

In the art of editing, the building block is the footage, and finding the statue inside it is the real key. It is common knowledge that while carving a statue, the first thing sculptors do is that they start with the edges, and the same goes for video editing. The first goal that an editor set is to carve the main shots into the best possible frame of the director's intention. During this stage, the editor cannot run wild with the material, the process of tweaking or finalizing comes later in the process. You must start with the edges, putting every single shot roughly into the timeline to create a preliminary version.

While roughly shaping a scene, it is important that you understand the flow of the story and what the script is trying to tell you. There should be a clear, narrative action in your scene which heavily relies on matching screen directions, temporal relations, and positions from shot to shot. Your scene should support the assumption that time and space are adjacent to successive shots. Therefore, every shot should be selected methodically while being careful that you are not missing any script line or changing the order of any dialogue that might disrupt the continuation. Another thing you should focus on is that you are including all the coverage needed to outline the scene. Meaning that you must add at least one instance of each angle, appropriate camera shots, and the specific planned shots such as dolly shots or rack focus shots into your time line.

The coverage includes all the camera angles used to film a shot. And it is the first place to look when you are searching for the director's intentions. The coverage of films and television is distinctly different from each other. In television series, what we mostly see are classic wide shots, close–ups, and over the shoulder shots. This is mainly because, in television, time is scarce. The directors have more or less only a few days to plan and execute the shoot. Similarly, editors also have a much lesser amount of time to work on their edits. Therefore, they adhere to a standard style that they use in the shooting and editing of every single episode. So, to save time and effort, the shows are designed and edited in such a way that one episode does not look much different from another episode. You might have noticed that in sitcoms, only certain camera angles are focused such as in a very popular TV show Friends where the entire series was recorded in front of the live audience.

Whereas in films, coverage is relatively different. Directors and editors have months to plan the shoot and the edit. You can utilize that time carefully to map your edit. Plan it in your head, put in on paper, or anything that you think can help you organize your thoughts. Manipulate your shots to give meaning to your scene and provide the audience with a truly unique experience. This is especially true if you want your scene to be narrative. Choose the shots that can effectively complement the script or actor's business. This way, you can determine which shots and camera angles which will best justify your narration.

Some words you need to focus on while placing and crafting your main shots are business, geography, and pillar shot. The business indicates your character's movements. Anything that a character does to communicate in a non-verbal way. It can include a smile, a wave, a simple hand gesture, etc. Geography means a character's location in a shooting space. And pillar shot is a shot with a clear intention that gives actual meaning to the scene.

While editing and combining a rough scene, you need to know which camera angle, frame, or focus goes with the script guidelines. For instance, wide shots should be used where there is a need of specifying the location, geography, and big business (in case certain movements of character are needed to be captured i.e. standing up from sitting or walking across the room). Close-ups on the other hand should be used as the main shots to convey emotions. I advise you to save these shots for powerful, emotional moments. Because when the audience can see defined features of your characters during emotional or important scenes, then an instant connection is created that hooks the viewers to the screens. Pillar shots are used to highlight moments that are crucial to the story. And some shots that are so incredibly filmed that they become defining moments in the scene can also be termed as pillar shots.

I remember there was this scene in the movie The Master where Freddie Quell was lying on top of the boat, cruising in the middle of the ocean. Whenever I look at the shot, I just keep wondering about the ideal composition of this scene. The perfect triangle of the deck, high details, and the difference between the sizes of Freddie and other soldiers just make this scene a perfect pillar shot. Another example is Darren Aronofsky's Black Swan, the scene where Nina just falls on the stage after her performance. The shot is filmed on Super 16mm, capturing the sense of bliss that the actor feels while falling. This shot was different from other shots of the scene with its handled style, symmetry, and especially slow-motion effects. While watching the scene, I felt a visual contrast that can communicate emotions and connect with the audience on some other level. These kinds of pillar shots can become lasing and meaningful images. The aesthetically pleasing shots always create a stir among the audience and represent the ingenuity of the filmmaker.

When you are cutting your master shots together to form a scene, you do not need to be so precise. Do not waste too much time finessing or you may defeat the purpose of the rough cut. However, there are certain things that you can do such as normalizing or compressing dialogues that will make a huge difference later. Another thing to keep in mind is that you do not need to attach music tracks if it will be scored later. You can simply prepare your cut without the music of any kind. Firstly, it will save you a lot of time and eliminate the possibility of the director or client disliking the scratch music which can sometimes inhibit them from properly judging the cut itself. In cases where the music or soundtrack has already been selected, there is no harm adding that into your cut. Similarly, try to be cautious about scratch narrations. If you must add it, then make sure that the voice is as clean and clear as it would be if a professional artist were doing it.

The initial draft of a scene that you have created will merely provide information for further processing rather than telling how good an editor you are. So, the feedback it will give you will mostly be about the story arc, actor's performance, and how scenes were shot. After preparing this draft, the questions that will come to your mind will be:

*   If the length of this scene is too long, how the shots can be trimmed without damaging the story?
*   If the length of this scene is too short, what shots can be further extended to justify the story?
*   If the length is perfect but the pace is misfit, how to compensate for it?

By focusing on these questions, you can plan your next moves in the editing process. In short, by assembling main shots into a rough time line, the editor and director can figure out the loopholes in the story along with the story flow and the time span. Utilizing this information, the editor can decide what parts should be trimmed or removed altogether, and what parts should be extended to meet the length objective. The sound and picture are usually not touched during this stage because these are the polishing touches that can be adjusted later. This assembly is created just for information and mostly it is not viewed after it has served its purpose.

Furthermore, to create some of the greatest scenes, it's necessary that you pay attention not only to pillar shots but to simpler shots as well because every single one of them will have an impact on the overall chemistry of the scene. You must select shots that deliver your message. When delivering a dialogue scene and your main aim is to represent what the characters are saying, you might start with the two-shot to establish the scene which represents the environment. Add alternate close–ups of every person who is talking and add reaction shots only when there is enough time flexibility or an extreme need to show what the other person is thinking. You can also use cutaways to highlight every element of the surrounding environment.

The stark example that I find of a perfectly balanced scene is from the Card, Cads, Guns, Gore, and Death directed by Ron Howard. I am not going to say that this movie is a Hollywood masterpiece. But the scene certainly has some very balanced shot selections. The scene basically revolves around three kids donned in western attire and playing a poker game. At one instance, one kid lays down his cards and motions to celebrate his victory when the other kid stops him and puts down a stronger hand. And then, in the heat of the moment, an argument erupts where the first kid calls the other one cheater. The third kid, who is played by the young Clint Howard, takes none of it and shoots the first kid. It all seems okay until a kid in a black hat comes from behind and shoots Clint in the back. And then we are left with a scene of bloody poker chips and bodies lying around.

What I find most interesting about this scene is that every shot is placed very carefully. It starts with an establishing shot which is a close-up of lying poker chips, then there is a tilted scene of the first player sitting on a chair. The fact that this scene was filmed by a fifteen-year-old is the most elementary thing about it, and this opening is indeed the best when I compare it to most of the older indie films I have watched. The rest of the shot is comprised of one take as it moves towards the second player, then again a glimpse of the chips, then to a bottle from which the third player takes a sip, and then it finally moves back to the first player who throws some chips into the stack. The whole thing is basically a tracking shot that introduces every character with all the props used in the scene.

From the first shot of the player, smiling and showing the audience that he has the best hand to the last shot of a lone poker chip drifting in a pool of blood, everything was perfectly synchronized. This scene was released as a bonus feature on the DVD of The Missing. I watched every feature of this scene very thoroughly because it is rare to see famous filmmakers like Clint Howard release their early work. I believe that this scene can aspire beginners to understand the dynamics of selecting master shots. However, it is much more complicated these days with various angles, frameworks, focus, and camera movement to approach shot selection. But it is something that defines the editor's creativity.

Chapter 8 The Initial Trim

Following the formula of shot, scene, and sequence, we have come down to the sequence part. In earlier stages, I have described how the master shots are selected and put together to craft an idea of the rough scene. I don't pay too much attention during that stage to the actual continuity or the proper flow of the clip. The main idea of putting shots together is to get the gist of the entire sequence. Those short time lines comprised of different shots to make up a scene help me get a sense of how the story line is flowing along with a sense of what technical errors, trimming requirements and other problems are awaiting me.

During the stage of initial trim, I work more on the time lines that I have created earlier and convert them into more sensible pieces that can later make up the initial sequence, or at least a road map, so to speak, from beginning to end.

Most video editing software exploits the feature of a non-linear time line, also sometimes called an NLE. Using this feature, you can add media, arrange it, cut it, or manipulate it in whatever way you think is the best. You can stack things up, down or in just about any way that you want to work, creatively speaking. You can alter the clips to make it sound, look, and feel the way you want it to. In nonlinear editing, there is no need for you to add media in sequential order, it is completely based on your editing comfort. You can start from the middle clip, then add the last clip, and later fill in with the appropriate shots.

Some of the most basic components of video editing software are time lines, tracks, play head, and media. time line is a flow of shots stacked together horizontally showing the footage on the right after presenting the footage on the left. To indicate the location of each frame, the time lines have time-code markers to make the task easier. Tracks, on the other hand, are usually assembled vertically consisting of the media (audio and visual) that will be added to the video time line. The media is something that rests on the time line and is comprised of images, visuals, audio, text, etc. The play head is also an essential element of the video as it depicts at what point in the video you are previewing.

There are many other features in NLE software that can help you formulate your initial time line efficiently such as splitting, cutting, zooming in, zooming out, track locks, and more. The location and the working of these features depend on the video editor you are using.

There can be various approaches through which you can arrange your time line. You should determine what suits your working comfort best before diving into the process. If I talk about myself, I always start with gathering all usable shots, as I have already discussed in the previous chapters. While gathering compatible shots, if you are unsure about certain footage that whether you need it or not, I advise you to still add it. If you are working on a big project and have a pile of footage to work on, label everything. This way, it will become easier for you to locate things later. Once you have all the key shots gathered, start adding them one by one into your time line. Do not worry about the order while adding the shots, you can figure out what goes where later once you have finished adding all the important shots. When everything is added to the time line, you can start your initial trim. The main purpose of trimming the clips is to narrow them down into usable pieces that correspond with the flow and the order of the story. I often create a giant time line consisting of way more than I plan to use. This way I can try lots of different things simply by turning clips on or off. If I like it I will make a sub–clip to watch later. Sometimes I create something just to scrap it because a later piece is stronger without the sub–clip I made. But once again, I never curtail a creative tangent. I let it play out even if it just gets scrapped later.

Trimming the shot length can also have diverse effects on your overall edit. It greatly impacts the attention span of the audience. I believe that attention is necessarily voluntary. What that means is that no matter how hard we try to focus our attention on something, we have these natural instincts to waver. The attention span of humans flakes out every few seconds, fluctuating in and out forming a natural pattern. If we relate this to a movie scene, you might have noticed that long shots sometimes become boring to watch. When perspectives keep changing within every few minutes, it keeps the audience more fastened to the screen.

I once read that patterns of shot duration throughout the movie has observed a great change over the past years. Shot durations are now designed in a way that it makes the movie more compatible with the natural fluctuations in human attention. Every new shot is trimmed and placed in such a way that it demands re-orientation of the viewer's attention. A video with only long cuts jumbled together might cause the audience's attention to waver. There should be a right mix so that the viewers stay engaged and completely lose their attention in the movie. For example, in Star Wars: The Empire Strikes Back, you will notice a tempo of short-take action sequences split by the moments of relative serenity.

If we talk about film noir, for instance, it is a relatively old style where you will see the sequence of longer takes that do not match with the instinctual attention span of humans. Most of these films were low budget runs made in the early 40s or 50s where directors relied mostly on long shots. Whereas, today, film making has evolved to something different and something relatable, where there is a way to show the audience a single scene from various viewpoints. Editors, these days, have a mountain of shots to work with, allowing them to trim and cut shots together in more extraordinary ways. Due to new cutting techniques, videos mesh better while taking into consideration the natural ebb and flow of human attention. But never forget that you are controlling the attention. Sometimes you want the attention to slightly waver so you can make an impact when you grab it back.

Many editors trim shots short inside a time line using Autodesk. They can start by trimming frames from head or tail. What I mean by head is the first source frame that is to be used in the shot, and similarly, the tail is the last source frame. They may even specify the number of frames they want to trim away from either the tail or the head. I almost never do that. I am a feel editor. I want the cut to feel right. I have a variety of ways I do it. Often it is in rhythm of some kind. It may be pulse of the scene, or the beat or just in rhythm with how the character moves or acts. But I almost always cut to a rhythm in my head. Sometimes I leave a little longer tail, or come in early. Once again, its feel that I prefer to technicality.

However, one thing to remember that you must remain conscious about leaving handles, as you cannot add a greater number of frames than the existing handles. Moreover, you can also not trim the specified shot out of existence. For removing any shot, you will have to delete it with the delete shot button

To shape out your time line perfectly, cutting your shots effectively is the key. How well you can utilize the tools to cut your shots reveals a lot about your editing abilities. As an editor, I pay a lot of attention to create meaningful sequences that complement reality. Once I roughly make my time line, I search for unintended distortions or interruptions that can be removed by cutting or trimming.

Almost every NLE has the tools for editing cuts. These are specially designed to help you craft a story and knowing what type of cut will make your work better can drastically change the quality of your video. One of the most essential and basic cuts that I use is The Standard Cut. I can easily term this as the most used cut out there, and that is why it is called "the standard". It also goes by the name of Shot–Reverse–Shot and is mostly used to generate a continuation in your edit from a different angle. You can use it to bring two different shots together or to staple the dialogue sequences. In a way, if you have ever placed two different camera shots together, you have used a standard cut.

Traditionally, these kinds of cuts utilize the one–eighty–degree rule where the eye lines of two characters match with each other. For example, when two characters are having a conversation where one character is shown looking at another character (off–screen), and then the shot changes showing the other character looking back at the first character, this is the shot–reverse–shot utilizing the 180–degree rule. This way, the audience automatically assumes that they are looking at each other.

The basic elements of the shot-reverse-shot sequence stem from the three-camera setup. The primary shots that you need are usually a two-shot of the character often in a medium or wide shot and the separate over the shoulder shots of both characters A and B.

This cutting technique perfectly complements the classic editing style of Hollywood. It typically provides continuity in the scene and maintains eye contact between the characters and the audience. With this cut, you can immerse your audience in the dialogues and the story rather than the visuals. Being simple, shot reverse shot never calls attention to itself from the editing perspective, and that is why sometimes, I refer to it as the "invisible editing". However, nowadays, editors are unearthing ways in which the standard cut can become dramatically enhanced, and a little more pronounced.

The model example that I find of shot reserve shot is in the Hard Fight in which Thomas Anderson made his feature debut. The film uses the establishing shot of a diner, a classic setup for one on one conversation scenes. The scene starts with the actor Philip Baker Hall directly looking at the camera, emphasizing his character's earnestness and positive intentions. Anderson, on the other hand, holds the audience's attention on the overall interaction while slightly breaking up the fourth wall. The scene uses a typical combination of over–the–shoulder shots with medium two–shots to engage the audience back and forth with the intensity of the conversation.

While cutting a conversation scene that uses shot–reverse–shot, I will emphasize one thing that the reaction shot of a character, to whom, a dialogue is being said is just as crucial for story building as the shot of the character who is speaking. To cut the scenes effectively, you must make sure that you understand all the nuances of the story and the beats of the conversation. This will help you evaluate when to cut to dialogue and when to reveal the reactions. It is of crucial significance because the reactions convey emotions, and the emotions in return allow the characters to connect with the audience.

Another important cut in the editing process is the Jump Cut. There are two types of this cut: bad and good. Meaning, the one that looks good in the edit and the one that does not look good in the edit. For instance, the one that does not look good is somehow unsettling and often cut the actor's dialogue. But these days, the jump cut has been transformed into something that makes the process of contracting a long take easier. The best way to use this cut is to string it with some kind of background soundtrack. Another cut that essentially finds its use in video editing is the J–Cut. It connects two shots that naturally would not go together. The way I typically use this cut is that I take the audio tail of the second shot and let it slip into the first shot. By doing so, you will see a stark resemblance to the alphabet J in your time line.

It helps to engage the audience into the next clip before it even makes a screen appearance.

Next is the L-cut which is the opposite of the J-cut. What it does is that it connects the audio from the first clip by extending it into the tail clip. This cut proves effective in the dialogue-loaded scenes as it breaks the tedium of the shot-reverse-shot. The L-cut also enables you to show the instant reactions of the characters to the audience.

Whenever you are working on an action sequence, utilize the Cut on Action. It is necessary for an action sequence to blend the shots as seamlessly as possible. To do so, you can assemble two clips by placing a shot of action moment in between. It makes your edit look seamless and tricks the audience into overlooking the cut in place. Cut on Action is the perfect choice for assembling a fight or chase sequence. Moreover, a crosscut breaks the sequence into two separate perspectives. For example, if you want to show two different narratives in the same scene, you do that by taking in shots from different viewpoints and melding them together by cutting between each. This way, the audience will connect with both narratives as you are showing them in "real-time"

You can also use cutaways in your edit to build tension, control time and space, and let viewers get into the character's head. It is a cut where the scene moves from the main action to any sort of visual information and then moves back to the original main shot, but with a new meaning. Visuals shown in a cutaway can occur anywhere in a specific scene and have no geographical restrictions. It is also necessary for your cutaways to be seamless in a certain situations and editing perfectly seamless cutaway is not always a piece of cake. It is mainly because sometimes, cutaway acts as the Band-Aid for poorly shot scenes, and editing in such a way that it does not generate any glitches can often become tricky. Furthermore, cutaway can also be used as establishing shots to showcase the character's location. When you are using cutaways as establishing shots, make sure not to dawdle too long or you might lose the viewer's attention.

Another widely used cut is montage. It comes especially in handy when you want to fast forward time. It is a great way to represent the passing of time, or a growth period by adding in a series of clips showcasing your character's growth.

Although the trimming or cutting of the shots is a meticulous process, the initial trimming stage only focuses on creating a preliminary outline. The tightening of footage and the final trim comes later in the process where an editor applies all the immaculate skills to drive the edit towards completion.

Chapter 9 Tweaking It Down

In previous chapters, I discussed how editors narrow down the footage with the initial trim to prepare a sequence that makes sense. Then comes the stage tweaking down some specific elements of the footage to drive it towards completion. It includes the application of various techniques that will give your edit a thorough look. Final trimming and tightening of footage and audio come first in the process and then transition and motion graphics. In this chapter, I will try to go through each element and describe how I tweak down my edit with the help of various techniques.

First things first, the term that is the heart of a perfect edit is cutting. Many editors struggle with the art of aggressive cutting. They either leave unnecessary scenes in the edit because they seem too cool or they leave extraneous soundbites because they sound touchy. And it is essential to understand the art of aggressive cutting because it is something that enhances the quality of your final edit. In the previous chapter, I discussed different kinds of cuttings and where they serve their purpose. But another very important thing are the objectives you need to keep in mind while tightening your edit. One thing that I find of utmost importance is knowing your audience before sitting down to tweak your edit.

I believe that to craft a great edit, two things are important. Number one, you need to realize where your audience's attention lies within a frame. Number two, you must figure out what your audience is going to feel at every minute and second of your frame. To master any edit, these two skills are very essential. I personally recommend if there is any moment in your footage that makes you unsure about whether it will catch your audience's attention or not or you are confused about what the audience might feel, then either alter it or make a cut. Do not leave room for fat in your final edit. This is a timeless tip because it provides an editor with a baseline from which to work. Ask yourself two simple questions and if the answer is no, then figure out the solution.

Another objective to keep in mind while tightening footage is to protect your story line. It is important because to grow as a storyteller, an editor must learn the discipline of cutting out every redundant item that does not fit in the story or is unable to convey the right message.

As an editor, you will have to face some tough decisions during the editing procedure, and sometimes it is crucial to defend the alternatives that you have selected. I suggest that you revisit the script while making key decisions but do not ignore the story that was filmed. This is critically very important because as you go through your edit and make cuts to tighten your footage, referring to the story will help you justify your choices. Focus on why and how your decisions are a perfect fit for the overall story. Also, keep in mind that the version of the story that is on paper is often very different from the captured version. So, you need to prepare yourself to meld these two versions together to create a third one that rightly communicates with the audience.

Another most important thing is to cut the fat from your footage in a way that it leaves only the relevant material. A piece of advice that I want to give is that cut your footage as short as you can, and then for a final trim, cut them down some more. I always follow this advice that someone gave me a long time back. My work often requires trimming down hours of footage into just a few minutes of sequence. To do so, I must be aggressive to tighten the final edit. That means that every soundtrack, every clip needs to be just of the right size and in the right order. In short films especially, the more fat I leave the greater is the risk of losing the audience's attention.

While approaching an aggressive cut, you must detach yourself from the politics of the entire job. This will help you tell a better story that is true to the audience's heart. After you get feedback from your clients, you might have to add some of the fat back into the edit but if you are positive about your choices, then you should prepare yourself as an editor to defend your cuts.

I remember doing one edit for a film called "In Search Of The Haunting". All through the final edit we had it timed at a certain spot. It had a pretty good flow. Suddenly the director told me the wanted to try and enter the film in a film festival that had a hard time limit on the length of the films. I remember struggling with how I would cut around 16 minutes out of the film. I went through the film looking for some of the things I liked, but were not really needed in the film. There were some scenes with cool editing tricks. There were things I liked because of my color work. Maybe I kept something because of how it took the attention from one scene to another. But in the end I cut out a ton. And you know what? The director loved it. Not only that, I did too. And after watching it a few times, I forgot about everything I had cut. It had great rhythm and it became clear that this was no longer the short cut. But it was the only cut. Sometimes its worth the exercise of doing a drastically aggressive cut just to see what happens.

I am listing some of the tips that I think are most helpful while approaching an aggressive cut. These are coming straight from my experiences:

* The first thing that should be in an editor's mind is that every frame counts. While editing, I try to be detailed by trimming off individual frames to save every fraction of a second that will comprise the five, six, or twelve-minute video.

* Cut out redundant sentences that do not make sense or are clearly not important. If you are editing a short video of an interview, try cutting "uhs" and "ums" because you have very little time, to sum up, the entire interview, and these pauses will be considered fat.

* Try to cut repetitive dialogues. Let us take an example of a series interview in which more than one person is being interviewed about a certain topic. Inevitably, at some point in an interview, two different people might be talking about the same thing. In that case, what you can do is cut off the similar points and add a different aspect by stringing some points together to make a stronger one.

* You must figure out beforehand what specific length you are going to aim for. For a web promo, I vouch for 2–4 minutes of run time. For TV commercials, there is a strict rule of only 29.5 seconds of run time. In Hollywood movies, studios are also very committed to a specified running time. Committing to a specific

length of time will always help you plan your cuts properly.

* When I start tightening the footage, I duplicate the versions at different stages, then rename them sequentially. I often use numbers such as promo 1, promo2, etc. Each subsequent footage allows me to be as aggressive as I want to be with my tightening procedure because I know that I can always go back if I mess up the trim.

* As I have mentioned earlier that you must be mindful of the message you are conveying. Always keep the clear message and motive of the piece in your mind. Every soundtrack and visual should contribute to the story. And if it does not make sense, cut it.

* You can split up the videos into multiple parts if you feel that certain information is important for the video but adding it might disrupt your run time. For my clients, I always prepare a bonus shorter video that includes clips that I felt were good but could not make in the final edit because of the video length. And

think of it this way, you can present it as a special feature to your audience if they want to delve deeper into the topic of the video while maintaining the run time and keeping the original video tight.

The tweaking stage also includes redesigning and modifying the soundbites and tracks. When it comes to creating an inconspicuous edit, sound design is the most important element to look at. Your audio tracks can make or break your entire edit. While tightening the audio, the first thing to remember is that every single frame needs to have an audio crossfade. It means that you must string two clips together to create a seamless flow. If it is not done properly, then you will hear hisses and unwanted pops when you run a sequence. Therefore, every clip needs to crossfade. To effectively carry it out, you need to listen to each fade attentively. When you are stringing two shots together, you must make sure that both shots have a few seconds of silence at the start and end.

You also must be careful that sound does not bleed into the next clip because it often happens in the crossfade. Try listening to the audio carefully with the headphones on. Another thing that you need to remember is that you should keep the room tone always at the ready. If the client forgot to record the room tone, you can search for some sounds online. But if you have a recorded room tone, then I will suggest that you always go for the authentic one instead of searching the internet.

To record an authentic room tone, simply place the recorder for 30 seconds to one minute in a room where you are filming. The tweaking stage always requires you to add a unique room tone into every scene. These are basically unnoticed sounds such as the whizzing of an air conditioner or a fan. Once you collect a clear room tone, paste it on the scenes and crossfade each cut accurately. This way, you will have a backdrop for all the sounds and your cuts will be less obvious.

Now, let us move to another important element of this stage which is working with motions. If we talk about motion graphics, it is a unique art that requires a lot of dedication and time from an editor. Blending graphic design with animations and crafting something that conveys the right emotions to the audience is not an easy procedure. I specifically want to mention one application named After Effects (AE) which is a staple program that helps in creating motion graphics. I will mention some of the tools that I find helpful when I am working with motions.

Before initiating any motion graphics project, you need to render out your sequence. Surely, this can be time-consuming, but it is an effective technique when you are using AE. Tight footage and trimmed layers will help you move forward faster. The second thing is to create animated paths which is something that you must have seen a lot in motion graphics. This tool is relatively faster. After Effects makes this technique very easy for you. AE provides you with various ways to approach this kind of effect. One way that you can do it is to establish key frames at each point on the pathway. However, the second way is even faster. You can also utilize one of the many animations presets present in the AE to carve a great animated path and get the desired results. Moreover, it will only require two essential key frames, at the start and the end.

You also need to understand the use of pixels and vectors if you want to master the art of motion graphics. There is a wide debate about whether you should use pixels or vectors. As you may already know, illustrator is vector based and Photoshop is pixel-based. It somehow depends on the scenarios because some features demand the use of pixels and others the use of vectors. For instance, when you are working with gradients, it is best to use pixels because there will be a lot of banding and the result will be much smoother. On the other hand, with other graphic elements, vectors are more widely used over pixels. For example, when working with animation projects where the camera is close, you will notice one thing that both types of graphics will create a blurriness. However, vector graphics can fix it to some extent by establishing the Continuously Rasterize feature. While with pixel graphics, this issue can not be fixed. To understand the complete dynamics of motions, it is important to realize when to use pixels and when to use vectors. Before jumping into the project, take your time to figure out what aspect of your design will demand the use of pixels and what aspect will demand the use of vectors.

When working with motions, you also need to check your key frames. Like any other type of animation, motion graphics also require the addition of key frames to incorporate movements. Speaking for myself, I rely on Graph Editor in AE to get the best possible results. Since motion graphics is all about animations, most of the animation rules can be applied to it. When you develop key frames in the time line, you will get the linear and unattractive movements. You can utilize the Graph Editor to manage your animations and create something that looks realistic and interesting. What Graph Editor does is that it allows you to spot the interpolations between key frames. You can efficiently create ease-in and ease-out by tuning the animation curve in the editor.

Another tool that is very helpful in creating graphic motions is the puppet tool in After Effects. It lets you set points on a still graphic that can be manipulated to present an animation. This tool is most effective when your subject is a human or an animal. What you can basically do using the puppet tool is that you can place all joints on a still graphic and make it manipulate those points individually on other graphic.

To start setting points, you can go to your toolbar and select the Puppet Pin Tool. You can then start pinning your subject in the places where there are joints. If your subject is a human, then pinning places will be wrists, knee, elbow, etc. Once you are done placing points, you can start manipulating those points to create whatever pose you want. You can also establish key frames like you do in animations. While this tool might not give an extremely realistic result, it is an effective way to move parts of your image without separating elements in different layers.

Another aspect of final tweaking can be transitions. The cut, the fade, and the wipe are all parts of video editing transitions. Transitions refer to joining two clips together in a most proficient way. Nowadays, there are plenty of video editing programs that offer a large library for built-in transitions. Not only that, but you can also buy fancier transitions to give your edits a more professional look. And on top of that, many applications let you design your own unique transitions.

In film making, you can create a whole feature film by just using cuts. But fancy transitions exist because they lend style to shorter videos that enhance the audience's interest. You can utilize them in short social-media videos and commercials but that does not imply that you cannot create short content without transitions. If you are creative, rules can be mended.

The trend of transitions keeps changing just like fashion. What is acceptable now, may not run next year. In the 70s and 80s, most TV shows utilized wipes, but now, it is not that widely used. Therefore, the more classical and fancier use of transition is more in demand these days. As an editor, it is important to understand the appropriate use of transitions because it is an important part of the editing process.

Chapter 10 Color Correction

We have observed in films an almost dark, eerie, and chilly blue tint that drives the overall theme of a project. These diverse hues create atmospheres that stand as monuments in a movie. As an editor, I believe that playing with color requires a lot of research and practice. To create a perfect scenario, you need to have advanced precision. Two major steps of the whole coloring process are color correction and color grading. Color correction is done to fix technical issues in footage to make it appear more realistic and natural. The main idea is to make the footage fine to the point that it looks clean and real, just like it would to the human eye. Color grading, on the other hand, is also technical but it lies more on the creative side.

The color grading process is more concerned with emotions and motives. With color grading, you can add colors to your footage in unnatural and new ways.

In the post-production process, the results are always a combination of both color grading and color correction. So, it's not one versus the other. Rather, it's more like a mix to generate better, more powerful results.

To start your coloring process, the first thing you need to do is specify your picture profile. It refers to a set of parameters that identifies the characteristics of your clip. For example, pro picture profiles that are used for videos are C-Log (Canon) or S-Log (Sony). Apart from that, many other profiles are also widely being used.

If your footage is shot in a RAW format, you will have clear control over image characteristics. Beyond its generally good quality, it is the main advantage of working with RAW. But one drawback is that it eats up a lot of space because the images captured are uncompressed and untreated. Contrarily, if you are not working with the RAW format, then the preferable is to record in a flat picture profile because it will allow you to later enhance and color your footage. Your picture profile can be shaped in whatever way you want, but if kept flat, it can generate more chances for you to step into a dynamic range and keep your footage smooth. These picture profiles give you a fair chance of controlling your images.

Once you have chosen your picture profile, you can begin with your color correction process. Color correction often includes adjusting white balance, contrast, and exposure to give your footage a very seamless and accurate look. With color correction, you can ensure that the successive adjustments that you have made are precise and not messing with the quality. The other purpose of color correction is to maintain visual consistency and make sure that everything has an accurate flow. Often with coloring, if your white is not properly white, any modification will make your image erroneous. If you go different, something that is as per your taste might not look good to somebody else. I always see working with colors like singing a great song. If every tone is not right, it may sound like I am playing with an out-of-tune guitar.

A micro-step in a color correction process that many editors find essential is applying an input LUT which stands for "lookup table". An input LUT is applied to move colors in your footage to a wider standard spectrum of HD television. This means that we keenly push our footage into this programmed adjustment to make it appear more perfect during the grading segment. But on the other hand, an output LUT is applied to give your footage a more cinematic look.

If we talk about Adobe Premiere Pro, the Rec. 709 LUT will ensure that all your color correction tools such as curves, scopes, sliders work the way they are intended and extract the most out of your images. Regarding color correction tools, I'm goint to share a quick metaphor. Let us assume that you are making a coffee. You always pour hot water over the beans; you never pour coffee over beans to make coffee. Similarly, the log footage is your hot water and the grounded coffee beans are your input LUT. The point is that you never pour already prepared footage having sharp characteristics over an input LUT because it will muddle up the entire quality by pushing it to an extreme level.

Rec. 709 will always ensure that there is accuracy, but it will not facilitate you to achieve the look you want, and this is where additional colors and LUTs will help you out. Applying a LUT to your footage will also give you an option of white balancing your image. You can either use Auto White Balance or make specific temperature alterations. Moreover, while shooting, you should make sure that your camera has been white-balanced, but since picture profiles usually mess up the color adjustments, you will have to readjust regardless. At this point, you mustn't apply any tints. Your focus at this stop should be to get as close to true white as possible. It is important to ensure that each step plays out correctly.

The next thing in the color correction process is to choose a home base clip. It is the best way to achieve visual consistency. Go through the mountain of footage and look for a base clip which has an average exposure level as compared to the rest of your footage. That way, you can easily set a standard and try to match things to a point that achieving a constant quality becomes possible. For instance, if you have a clip that has an extreme exposure throughout, you might face inconvenience creating a similarity between that footage and the others. It will create options for you to eliminate in a cut.

Another thing in the process is adjusting blacks and whites, and for that, you will have to use scopes. To even out everything, adjust the levels to reach the true black and white. Make sure that your footage appears properly adjusted in terms of white and black. You can achieve that look using several tools. Focus on the scopes as they will let you know if you have gone rough with the coloring levels. You will also need to make sure that your RGB curves are adjusted.

Then move towards another step which is adjusting the overall gamma of your footage. This is the stage where you can alter or adjust different elements of your image such as shadow, highlights, mid-tones, etc. We need to be subtle while doing it because, at this point, we are still doing corrections and have not entered the grading phase. The whole point of gamma adjustment and color correction is to fix things, not to make your footage look cooler or apply your imagination to it. Here, we are more concerned with color fidelity and making a relationship between intensity levels in the footage. Later during color grading, you can be a creative, rough, blow out your whites and blacks, etc. But for now, maintain coordination.

Another essential aspect is the secondary color correction. It primarily involves separating specific parts or elements of the footage within a specific frame and fixing only those. It goes something like that, just like we have created prototypes for characters, objects, and imagery which also have color schemes and color classification. It is obvious that the sky is blue, and the leaves are green. Now for instance, if you have a plant in your footage and its color looks weird, it will likely mean that the color correction is off and the audience will question your story. The point that I want to drive is that skin colors need to look real, the color of leaves need to look the way they generally are, and the environment must appear the way it is. The imagery that you portray feeds the suspicion of disbelief and that is why it is crucial in storytelling.

Now the step where you can start adjusting colors as per your visions is referred to as advanced color correction. During this step, you need to remember that you can adjust the colors while remaining on the "correct" side. You can boost the colors within your footage if you want to but be careful that it only needs to be a little adjustment of hues to specify the imagery. Otherwise, we still want to make things look the way they are. What I want to point at here is that you can begin to apply a little bit of your imagination in this stage.

I usually do not apply color correction tools on master footage, but I rather do it on small and individual pieces. First, I take a piece of footage from the scene and sequentially apply the required color correction tools to it. I typically work on color contrast and exposure first and then I adjust whites and blacks and register what color casts may appear. If the alterations that I have done in terms of color correction work out, then I copy those adjustments and paste it onto all the other pieces of footage that are either originated from the same camera, or just belong to the same scene. If you are working on the footage from different cameras of the same scene, then it is important to make sure that all the footage is adjusted similarly so that the scene looks even, without any differences. But in the case of scenes where there is a closeup of a face or something similar, then color adjustments can be different. Otherwise, I prefer adjusting all footage in the same style.

Color grading, the second step in the coloring process affects the tones and voices in the footage. This process can steer the whole persona away from the actual color of the scene. This step is utilized when color is needed to be used as a narrative mechanism. Creative color can play such a vital role in the overall narration that you can almost think of it as a character itself.

When you begin color grading, work with software that amplifies your editing abilities. You can either work with an NLE (non-linear editor) like Adobe Premiere Pro or any program that is specifically designed to adjust color grades within your video. Same applications can be used for both color correction and color grading processes, but as a professional, I usually prefer different software for each process.

The basics tell us that every piece of recording has its color grade, regardless of any later modifications that have been performed on it. The case is different for color correction because the shots that are not adjusted to a specified standard are not color corrected but every shot that has been captured holds a certain color grade. And during color grading, it is your job to emboss that grade to show your targeted look. This is something that differentiates the pros of editing from the noobs.

This is the stage where your colors will become your characters and will start telling stories. Color grade is something that makes your footage look stylized. This means that you can now start making the more artistic decisions. Regardless of whether you are using the same tools that you have used for color correction, you can add different layers to the footage to paint the entire work of art. Start shaping your video during this phase to explain that the grading process is additive. That means we are adding information with colors to something that is already soaked in color values. Remember that we are not to change the digital value of color, but rather pile some of our color values to the existing ones. What more you can do is add creative LUT to the footage that is already color corrected. This way, you can apply the entire color grade with a click.

One of the challenges that beginners may face with color grading is that what you see on the monitor is not always true. Often due to bad screen collaboration and ambient illumination, the overall video display can be altered to some extent. To ensure that your color grading and correction is precise, most professional editing software such as Avid, Adobe Premiere Pro and DaVinci Resolve offer solutions in the form of scopes. These panels give you a variety of information about your footage.

When you are in the color grading phase, vector scopes can make your work a lot easier. It illustrates what tones you are using and what are their saturations. Because the vectors scope analyzes the digital signals and is not influenced by any aspect that might disrupt your color grading perception. Once you master their use, they can guide you to the correct information.

Colors affect our psychology and filmmakers use this to play with the emotions of the viewers. With color grading, it is very easy to tweak each scene from a color standpoint and create a certain kind of mood. In horror films, darker colors are used in almost every scene, even the ones that are shot in the daytime to make viewers experience feelings of eeriness. Or sometimes, when you are watching an old Western show on TV, you might notice that most scenes have a hint of a yellow or sepia tone.

With colors, you are always free to create an emotional appeal that can hook the audience. If you are working on thc color grading of the scene where a character has died, and the death is sinister, then you might want to create scenes with darker hues, a little bit more contrast, and edginess. And if the character was endearing, and the death is just tragic, then hues of colors should be adjusted differently. For someone's death who was beloved, you might want to steer some tension away from the scene with a little less contrast and brighter hues. To further highlight the sad emotions, I sometimes soften the footage, usually, on the faces of characters who are delivering sad dialogues in the scene. So, for the most part, playing with colors to depict emotions is the most intricate portion of the whole editing process.

Once again, I will refer to the film "In Search of the Haunting". I think this was some of the most creative I have gotten with color grading. When I received the film, it was a standard color film. But there was something that spoke to me while I was watching it.

knew that this film would never have real impact in full color. So I initially turned it black and white.The director loved it. I then started playing around with adding blue hues and even some greens. I ended up creating an overall look that while it was still color based, it looked like a different type of black and white. I worked with this on each individual scene. I adjusted the color to fit the mood of each scene, while still giving the feel of black and white. Some scenes I even pushed the limits so the viewer couldn't quite tell if it was black and white or color. Maybe I would let the real color of a characters clothing be more visible than it had been. Or maybe I would insert a color frame or 2 that would generally go unnoticed, but would give a strange tension to the scene. I allowed the color to play as important of a role as a character in the film.

Another pretty cool piece of color work was, strangely enough also turning a color piece into a black and white piece. I did not do as much work with the black and white this time around. But what I did was allow only one color other than black and white to show. This color was red. The actress in the lead had a red tint to her hair. So in most scenes I had the red just slight. But there were a few scenes where there was an apple. There was also a scene with blood. In these scenes I allowed the red to be fully saturated. It accented a few things that really made the entire film come together. This was early in my career and it gave me an entirely new perspective on the power of color.

I also remember working on a film called "The Square Root of 2". This film had a classic mistake made in it. The DP had shot much of it with mixed light, meaning he mixed daylight and tungsten. This created an unnatural yellow hue throughout most of the film. This was back in the days before plugins were created to aid in this situation. I actually had to go into almost every scene and add varying degrees of blue to bring true white back. Admittedly, I was never able to make every scene perfect because each camera also did not have the same temperature. But I took the film from unusable, to watchable.

While color grading is more entailed than simple balancing, the choice somehow depends on your film budget as well. If you are an editor who is working on a low budget film, then only color balancing might be an option for you. Although it can be quick when you are working with the shots of a few cameras, the presence of more cameras can increase your workload. But as I have mentioned earlier in the chapter, you can work scene by scene and figure out what works well for your overall footage, and then copy–paste the adjustments. This trick can help you color balance your entire footage effectively and quickly.

Chapter 11 Audio

Audio post-production is a hugely important part of the video editing workflow. Although audio editors typically don't get famous for their work, in movies their job is the most crucial. Let us suppose that the screenwriter writes an amazing dialogue, but how can the audience get it if an editor does not tune it correctly? To build the scene and an aura, certain sounds play a vital role such as the rustling of leaves, whizzing of cars nearby, or ruffling of clothes, theses sounds make the audience realize that they are living in the scene.

For instance, in one of the scenes in the Batman movie where he was looking at the dark and silent alley from the rooftop of a building, we could hear the jumble of sounds. The cars rushing by, police sirens echoing in the distance, unknown voices of people on the street, etc. Then the Joker enters the alley with wailing and screaming Vickie Vale. At this point, we hear the crackle of Joker, muffled screams, and scratching of heels across the pavement. The scene again changes when batman dives headfirst into the alley. We hear a combination of whirring and ruffling of Batman's clothes. This is then followed by the fight, and we hear all sounds of punches, thumps, and grunts.

So, when you were watching this movie, it might have taken you only a few minutes to get past it, but as an editor, I know how much hard work there is behind this scene. Audio editors have to work hundreds of hours to make sure that every snippet of dialogue goes smoothly, every scrape of shoe sounds right, every minor detail of background noise fits in, and every sound effect blends perfectly. In this chapter, I will discuss different aspects of audio post-production. From audio mixing to foley, I will try to cover the basic fundamentals.

In film and television, audio recording is done separately from the video. This is because unlike your home camera, professional film cameras do not have built-in microphones. Therefore, all dialogues and sounds are recorded with either a boom microphone or tiny wireless microphones often hidden in the actor's clothing. Foley and ambient sounds are often added in the post-production stage.

In the post-production stage, editors finalize and assemble their work. I typically start post-production once I am done finalizing my locked cut. This cut contains all the crucial visual effects, main shots, graphics, transitions, special effects, etc. With my finalized locked cut, I sequentially start spotting my video for sound.

For dialogues, I examine every uttered sentence to notice discrepancies or badly recorded lines. I may reject dialogues if they are too loud, too quiet, non-comprehensible, or especially when the actor's voice does not synchronize with his lips. Then the next step is to identify where in the whole video you need to add external sounds like ambient noises. Then comes the part of Foley where I add detailed sounds of otherwise unnoticeable actions such as walking on the wood floor, the sound of putting a china dish on the countertop, a tap running, etc. Then I add music to the video. It can either be an originally composed piece or a copyrighted one. It depends on the client.

In films and television, if some dialogues are badly recorded, they can be re-recorded or replaced. The dialogue editor can ask the actors to come for an ADR (Automated Dialogue Replacement) session. This way, the editor, and actor work together to record better-synchronized dialogues. Editors record lines with on-screen lip movements and later mix the audio to smooth out the existing recording.

Foley and Ambient sounds are two different things. Foley artists, for instance, use tricks to produce sounds that are mostly very common such as the creaking of the door, a glass shattering, scratching off a wooden chair, etc. On the other hand, the ambiance is more concerned with natural sounds. Sound effect editors are responsible for collecting libraries of environmental sounds. For instance, they record sounds of heavy traffic on Monday and save them for appropriate video recordings. They record a fan whirring in an empty room, children playing, or a crowd of people hauling. The ambient sounds can also be purchased from existing libraries. But most movies use original recordings. In the original Star Wars movie, the sound effect for a roar of a tie fighter was a bellow from a hazy elephant. And remember the hum of the lightsaber? It was a fusion of a 35mm projector and a TV static.

The most essential part of audio post-production is the mix. This is where all the sound elements like pacing, ambiance, noise reduction, and sound effects go. In big projects, the post-production job is divided between various editors. But for smaller projects, the jobs of music mixer, dialogue editor, and effect designer are all performed by one or two people.

Most people think of audio mixing as a high-end work with giant audio consoles of more than 12 feet having so many knobs and faders that it can make your head twist. Those devices sure exist in movie studios, but that does not necessarily mean that you cannot do mixing without these professional, high-end instruments. If you are mixing from your home studio, it is more likely that you are using convenient software like Pro Tools, Garageband, or Logic. And what you do in this software is drag or fade. So, in the end, you are, pretty much, doing exactly what they do in the big studios. Some software, like Adobe Premier Pro or Avid actually have pretty robust audio mixing capabilities within them as well.

Think of audio mixing as a process of editing and balancing tracks to produce a blend of smooth and clear sound. When you mix your audio, always attempt to balance out the levels, so that all the instruments in audio can be heard at a specific volume. I am explicitly talking about songs here. This balance can be achieved by compression plugins. Another thing to keep in mind is that you should cover a wide range of frequencies. This way, the sonic palette will sound full and can be later improved with plugins and EQ effects. For dry audio tracks, go for effects such as modulation, distortion, and reverb. With the use of Auto–Tune or filters, mistakes that have occurred during the tracking stage can be removed. For instance, EQ can reduce the whining of guitar strings in the music mix.

I can generally say that audio mixing can be a process of trials and errors. You can improve only by learning and practicing. Coming from the music studio background I have, and having mixed more things than I can count, I have learned the art of mixing pretty well. Therefore, I will share some tips with you that I have found most helpful.

The first thing that you need to be clear about is panning your instruments. What most editors do while mixing is, they set all their instruments at the center of the stereo, and this is a mistake. What I would suggest is to pan your instruments to either the left or right of a sound stage. This will help you make the sound from each instrument clear and distinct to the audience.

The second thing is applying compression but be careful and do not overdo it. For music, compression can bring great depths but if overdone, it can dampen the tones to some extent. Compression works when the volume of the loudest beat is reduced, and the overall level of the audio is raised. This is an effective way of enhancing your quieter sounds and reducing the louder ones. But keep in mind, if you overuse compression, you will eventually lose the spark in your music. So, be wise and use it to the point where audio does not lose its distinctness.

The third thing you can do is add reverb. But remember that it can also muddy your mix. The best way is to add reverb during the mixing stage to very dry audio. This will result in the most creative illusions. You can add backgrounds of concert halls or spacious studios when the original shooting was done in an attic. But just like compression, you need to be careful with reverb too. Use it only where it will not destroy the overall aura of the audio. For instance, if a singer wants to convey a message in his lyrics, do not lose it in the reverb. Sure, you can create an atmosphere with it but do not lose precision while doing it.

Now, the fourth tip is to apply high-pass filters. Most EQ effects have built-in filter options and can be applied to cut off certain frequencies and make some individual parts higher. But again, I will advise that you use this technique in moderation and be subtle with it. While high passes can sound very cool in headphones, it can murk up the mix as well.

The final tip from me is to test your mix on different mediums. If you are using some high-end headphones to listen to your mixes, it can give minor details about your work, but be aware that most of your audience might not hear it on high-end equipment. Therefore, test in on different mediums like car speakers, stereo, earbuds, soundbars, and laptop speakers. That way, you will have clarity on how the audience will listen to your mix.

Elements of pacing are very important in audio post-production. Pacing is something through which we can control the audience's emotions and time in a narrative. We can manipulate what the audience would think with the pace of dialogues and sound. Speeding up or slowing down the audio can insert the effects of time narrative and create dramatic effects in the scene. If the scene is long, drawn-out, and frenetic, sound can play a vital role to make its pace a litter quicker. The absence of sound can affect the overall narrative. If in a scene, you want to create certain dramatic effects, you need to focus on your audio pace, the background music should be altered in a way that it represents the clear emotion. Moments of reflection in movies are generally shown with slower music. Contrarily, action scenes are filled with high paced sounds and music. Likewise, the pace also slows down for thrilling scenes. The structure of the scene can also represent its own pace.

When establishing scenes are shown, there is always a slow build-up. Then the pace picks up as the characters are shown fighting some obstacle. And when something disastrous happens, the pace that was picked up begins to slow down. Throughout the entire story, the pace keeps rising and falling to build up the tension and create dramatic and interesting turns. It is the most effective storytelling technique.

With the arrival of digital audio, we now expect more from our audios than we did in the past, and noise reduction is the key expectation. What we do in analog audio is shuffle tracks into other tracks and try to minimize the sonic impact of this action. Many strategies have been used in the past to lessen the effects of noise that mess up the analog audio. Today, various audio workstations can mix hundreds of tracks and the only problems that occur are either dreadful recordings or badly used filters. But fortunately, various techniques and devices are out there that can reduce the noise in the audio. Not only are these devices affordable but also provide high-quality results. Therefore, noise reduction in audio is not that big of a problem these days.

The main idea I have when I edit for noise reduction is, not harm. When you sit to reduce the noise in your audio, sometimes, doing just a little can be enough. Or it can be said that leaving a little bit of noise sometimes is fine. If you reduce noise a little too much, the audio might start sounding worse and artificial. So, always start with a gentle hand. Sometimes, filters can work on certain noises. Sometimes, denoisers need a couple of light passes to go away. Every case of noise would be different, and what to use will entirely depend on the situation. But the simplest way that I use is by applying an EQ. For instance, if there are hisses and pops and in your audio of let's say 10kHz, then low pass filters may be all you need.

Now, another important aspect of post-production is that sound design often provides an artistic input. For one thing, the sound effects used to finalize the audio are often build from scratch. The thing with natural sounds is that we would not want to hear every sound that is present in the shooting space, but even if it was possible to record every noise, it would not sound right in the patterns of a film. Sound is an element that is very subjective and highly depends on the visuals and the mood that set up the entire scenario. The soundtrack of the real natural environment is usually too dense to be added in films. In the real world, we humans select to focus on certain noises and filter out others. Similarly, for films, dialogue editors need to focus on which sound is more important and filter out the less important ones.

As an editor, you need to understand the emotions of the audience and create the element of tension, sadness, or joy with your sound effects. Walter Murch, the leading light of sound design, once quoted the character sounds as 'Coronus' that can magnify dialogues of each character and amplify their screen space. A character who is associated with a specific sound depicts that he or she has a real presence and is prevalent in the scene. In a way, even when the character is off-screen, his or her importance is pervasive.

Let's move towards ambient sound now. Every room, city, and place has its original sound. Our brains are designed in such a way that we often tune out ambiance to notice more important things. If you are indulged in a conversation, you probably would not notice all the minor noises around you. Birds chirping, children playing, leaves rustling or fountain ticking, chances are you would not pay attention to these background noises.

Quiet places also have an ambiance. If you are sitting alone in a silent room, there would still be sounds of fan whizzing or car horns outside. Similarly, when filmmakers edit their films, they focus on ambiance to make their idea of reality look truly "real". In movies, notice certain details when two characters are having conversations. If the scene has been shot inside a restaurant, only the dialogues are recorded live. The ambient sound is added later in the audio post to make everything look natural. Fortunately, for low budget projects where recording original ambiance can be a little time and money consuming, various websites offer libraries for ambient sound effects. If you are working on a restaurant scene, searching for "restaurant ambiance" will give you hundreds of entries. You can easily purchase or download these effects for your videos.

Chapter 12 Final Cut

In the previous chapters, I have roughly gone through the complete video editing work flow. I have shared my own experiences in terms of selecting appropriate shots, cutting and trimming them to fit the story line, playing with colors to control the audience's emotions, and manipulating audio to work with the overall flow of my edit. Now comes the final part. Once you are done editing your video, the most important thing is reviewing it for the client's satisfaction. Collect feedback from your other professional friends to make sure that you haven't left any unintentional loopholes in the video. Sit down with a pen and paper and run the whole video from start to end. Write down the things you observe, and work again on the video if you notice any discrepancy.

I have always believed that video editing is a complex process. With so many steps taking place sequentially, it is possible that you can make a mistake. Therefore, always keep some extra time before the deadline to give your video a final review. In this chapter, I will present my final thoughts on how you can proof run your video to spot any problems and make amendments if needed. I will also be talking about some video editing software that I generally use, and some final tips that can help you in a long run.

During the editing process, an editor can lose the edge and mess up the details because it is a long and draining task. It is important that you maintain sharpness all the way to the end. As a professional, I understand that when you commit to a long project, it is difficult to sustain the objective standpoint that you were following earlier. So, things become unclear, and you lose track. What were you doing? What is working out? What is messing things up? Have you missed something?

Keeping these questions in mind is very important. Especially so, when you are near the final stage of completion and things become challenging because you are unable to see where your work is going.

But fortunately, the most effective way to sharpen your edit is to see your work through someone else's eyes. This way, you will have clarity. And watching it with someone else will also transform your viewing experience. Suddenly, you will be able to figure out the unsettling cuts, confusing moments, long drags, and unwell audio tracks. Get your work in front of other professionals as early as possible because it is a rapid way to recognize where you lack and what things need to be reworked. Showing your edit to more than two people will let you see their reactions, and you will get an early realization about what the audience might think of your edit. That is why, during audience test screening, editors focus more on people's reactions rather than the video. It tells them a whole lot about their work.

The second thing you can do to evaluate your edit is to watch it without audio. Turning off the sound during the final screening is a trick that I frequently use. Many famous editors like Walter Murch and Joe Walker also observe this technique to evaluate their performance. I sometimes play with my edits without sound. I alter it as a silent movie because it is a unique approach where you can just work with visuals and figure out what is happening in the story. Doing this makes you really tough in your editing. The silent approach also leads you to the long–standing filmmaking axiom which says "Show, do not tell". It displays where you can make cuts between extraneous pauses, dialogues, or waffles. Just keeping your focus on the visuals will also help you configure individual shots and scenes with more accuracy since sound is not disturbing your overall perspective and not affecting the pace. You can understand this by thinking of an action scene, it will seem much slower if the music and background audio are not present. Another variation of this technique is running the video in black and white or flipping the whole image to shake up your vision. On the other hand, you can also go for an inverse technique of the previous one which is turning off the visuals during evaluation. By turning the image off, you can pay more attention to the audio of your edit and engage more closely with the entire pace created by the sounds. In a way, you will see your work in a completely different fashion. Particularly, when working with documentaries, this approach yields good results. You can even build an entire radio edit with this approach by just utilizing some original soundbites and moments. With documentaries, you can hit off the right idea by focusing on the sound because most of the story revolves around the audio narration and dialogues. Even in movies, and other videos, you can turn off the visuals to listen to the pace and discern where things are not working out. Pick up the problems with pace, non-clear dialogues, and understand what amendments are essential. This way, you will create a breathing room for imaginative ideas. With this trick, you will see a stronger sense of direction in your edits. I believe that this technique is very effective because it helps me judge the performance of sound effects and ambiance.

Sometimes when I finish a project, I'll evaluate its performance by running the whole edit first without the sound and then without the visuals. You need to do firm scrutiny of your entire edit to maintain a pace throughout and create a constructive landscape of shots. I have a trick for this. When you finish your video in good shape, take a slip of paper, and write down scene numbers on each slip. Then select a random one from a hat and review that scene thoroughly. Evaluate each shot and figure out if there are any holes or burns. Towards the end of the project, some later scenes are not often as worked out like the others. Reviewing each scene separately will allow you to work on any carelessness that might have happened.

I will advise you not to tire people by telling them your perspective. Rather, let the audience themselves invest their attention to the best moments and accuracy of your edit. Furthermore, the whole idea of randomly reworking each scene is to create a fresh standpoint on how each scene is affecting the story in seclusion. Even if your edit is not scene-based, try this trick by dividing your project into individual segments, mapping out the different portions of your edit, and then applying the same shuffle thing. Another major thing that affects the overall evaluation perspective is distance. If you are invested in a project for a long time, try putting it aside for a few days. I find it very helpful when I need to reconstruct my perspective. You will see your project with entirely different eyes after a few days of break. I remember reading a statement from editor William Goldenberg ACE. He said that he used to screen the movie at seven in the morning, and that was his everyday routine. He was losing his objectivity for the project, and twenty four hours of the break gave him a boost and allowed him to see what is happening from a different perspective. Sometimes, a break during long projects can become an objective faster for you. I can understand how draining long projects can be. Therefore, I advise that bringing some distance is the only shortcut to make things work. Taking a good break can renew your imaginative thinking. When you resume the work after the breaks, it seems newer and you look at it from an outsider's perspective. This works as a second opinion and lets you correct the mistakes you previously made. This decreases the probabilities of errors in your editing and makes it more fluid and persistent.

Now, moving on, I want to mention some editing software that I use for my videos currently or have used in the past. Adobe Premiere Pro, for instance, is the most widely used editing software and considered one of the best. Although, most professional editors believe it to be a good software for accuracy there are still many that do not use it. What software to use depends heavily on the editor's comfort and choice. The best-suited software for you might not fit with the working criteria of other editors. It also depends on the needs of your edit and your working skills. While Avid, and Premiere Pro are common choices of editors, Apple Final Cut Pro X is also in demand. All three have very high accuracy and are used by many Hollywood professionals. However, they differ in some functionality. One of the major differences between them is that Final Cut Pro is free of all subscription charges. So, if you use Mac and the idea of a creative cloud subscription does not suit you, Final Cut Pro X may be a good choice because you will have to pay only once. It also has some pro-level features such as a magnetic time line, effect options, grouping tools, and a precise and straight forward editing path. And in the latest version, I have also noticed advanced fixes that enable relatively fast work. But, for sure, both Avid and

Adobe Premier Pro each give you more tools and are much more precision oriented editors.

Another software that is a good little editor is Vidello Create. It is not suitable for heavy editing. But for creating and editing simple short social media videos Create yields some amazing results. Even non-professionals can create good edits by using prepared video templates. The software also has stocked up video clips, and copyrighted music tracks to use for free. For different social platforms, the application has different aspect ratios such as square, horizontal, or flat.

DaVinci Resolve is also used by many Hollywood professionals. This free video editing tool has been used for many big-budgeted movies and TV series. The most powerful feature of this software is its color correction tool and audio modifications. If your priorities in an edit are color grading or audio post, then DaVinci is the right fit for you. The software also gives you options of color featuring, facial recognition, and tracking. As audio fixtures,

DaVinci uses Fair light, an editing tool that creates a mix. All the important features are present even in the free version.

It's important for an editor to capture emotions and moments purposefully through his work. Editors know human psychology and how one might respond to certain scenes and clips. Editing is something that comes from experiences and a deep understanding of societal familiarity. Some closing tips that every editor needs to create a moving story of perfection includes numerous aspects. Everything is crucial, from camera angles to the actor's body language. Be an actor and observer at the same time to add the finish of reality in your editing. I prefer observing the content before I start editing. Different content needs a multitude of editing to go with the theme. For instance, the editing in a TED talk is minimal in comparison to the editing we must do in a narrative cut of a documentary. Maintaining continuity in your editing is essential to sustain a persistent flow of time and space throughout your video. There is a trick that I like to call invisible editing. Meaning that when you edit a clip, you need to highlight certain parts and pieces and fade out the others from the audience's attention. To summarize, you need to make invisible things visible in the most unnoticed and natural ways. Choosing the best camera angles is a basic part of video editing but selecting the right camera angle is much more important than choosing the best one. Think about what the audience would want to see in a particular moment to better comprehend the story. For example, if an actor is saying something to someone, then it's important to show how the other person is reacting to it. Facilitate effective shot selection to make the story more interesting and captivating. Try to take the seats of both audiences and the storyteller in turns to produce a self-explaining cut.

Close-ups and medium shots add more to the flow of a cut. You can use diverse camera angles between cuts to show the audience the landscape, weather, and time. In the clip where a story is being told, it's best to use close-up shots to display the expressions and responses of the actors. Medium shots help immensely in screening the precise body language of the actor, which is essential to specify the mood of the clip.

All speakers do not have the same rhythm and persistence to their voice and body language. Pay attention to the different voices, actions, and movements in a certain clip to capture all the significant aspects of a character through your editing. Sometimes the cut demands to capture every breath and each heartbeat which requires plenty of close-ups and sound effects. Understand and study the clip to bring out the best in each cut through the immaculate power of editing. Make your transition shots smooth and even, especially when you cut on a certain action or movement. The audience follows every movement from the beginning, through the transition, and to the next shot. The fluidity of an action conceals the editing, and the attention is concentrated on the action rather than the transition of the shot. Cutting on the action is an effective way to transition the clip creatively without breaking the continuity of the shot

Heavy consonants at the end of the finishing sentence can make the cut look more final and make the editing look less obvious and unnatural. Cutting on words requires a tone of finality near the end. Make the ending words ring more strongly to make them more memorable. You can extend the ring of the sentence to maintain the continuity of the shot and make it more persistent. Captivating the audience's attention is the prime objective of editing a clip in an engaging manner. Maintaining continuity in your editing is important to trap the attention of the viewers and keep the audience on the edge of their seats. Don't use similar camera angles, diversify your shot selection technique to preserve the fluidity of the story. One essential part of editing is soothing out the errors. Sometimes, the speakers use unnecessary words like "um" and "uh" while talking, especially if it's an interview. Cutting out the speaker's errors makes the shot clearer and more understandable. It feels more real and straightforward for the audience to comprehend without paying much attention to the pauses. I like focusing on the person who is talking and the one who is reacting to it. If the clip features numerous actors, then you need to see who is giving a worthy reaction to it and edit it midway to the sentence being delivered. This way you will be able to capture both the speaker and the listener.

Now the hardest part is knowing when to quit. At some point, you must simply choose that the editing is done. This is how editing is. It is never really done as there is always another tweak you see when you run it back. But at some point you simply declare it a final. It is done. It's the Final Cut. Print It!

Chapter 13 In Closing

I had no real idea what this book would be when I began writing it. I just started one day and ended another. While most of the words are mine, I do want to acknowledge that a small group of people did some of the writing for me where it came to some of the explanations of the editing softwares I do not use and a few other tecchnical things. First, I want to say that I will never do that again. It took more time for me to rearrange their writing than it would have for me to research, digest, and write it for myself. I did, however, leave in about 20% of what they wrote. So I apologize if there are times where it seems like my personality dropped out and someone else was speaking. That is exactly what happened. Why do I bring this up? Well, this is a book about editing. Is it not? I prefer the truth always.

I also wish to add a bit about something else that occurred to me while I was writing this book. I want to emphasize the importance of being who you are. I think there is far too much suffering in the world that is born out of people being afraid to simply be who they are. Don't be afraid. The world is full of people. Each of us are living our own lives. We deal with our own thoughts, perceptions, principals, guiding influences and secret desires. We follow our own spiritual beliefs. We live our own trials and tribulations. And yet, at the end of it all, we are all going through this human experience. And, each of us are unique unto ourselves. Yet, we tend to judge ourselves, often harshly, based on how others are dealing with their own experience of being human. This is quite natural. But it is the wrong focus – at least in my opinion.

None of us asked to be born. Yet, here we are. If we are here and we did not ask to be born that means we did not need to be born – for ourselves. If that is the case, we might ask ourselves "who needed me to be born?" In the end, we did not create ourselves. We, along with our entire universe (and beyond) are a creation outside of our own understanding. Our blood, for example, is made up of 13 elements. Yet you can not combine those elements and make human blood. They must combine at the exact and precise moment in order to exist as human blood and carry life. Similarly, the man and woman must come together at the exact time, in the exact space, and with the exact intention in order to perpetuate their existence. You were created for a reason. You were created for a need. And if that need is not yours, than whose is it?

Nothing is random. Be overly generous with your kindness and with your love.

Practice Gratitude.